THE
POETICS

THE
POETICS

Translated by
Theodore Buckley

ARISTOTLE

GREAT BOOKS IN PHILOSOPHY

Prometheus Books

59 John Glenn Drive
Amherst, NewYork 14228-2197

Published 1992 by Prometheus Books
59 John Glenn Drive, Amherst, New York 14228-2197.
716-691-0133. FAX: 716-691-0137.

Library of Congress Cataloging-in-Publication Data

Aristotle.
  [Poetics. English]
  The poetics / Aristotle ; translated by Theodore Buckley.
      p.   cm. — (Great books in philosophy)
  ISBN 0-87975-776-0
  1. Poetry—Early works to 1800. 2. Greek literature—History and
criticism—Theory, etc. 3. Literary form—Early works to 1800.
4. Aesthetics, Ancient. I. Buckley, Theodore Alois, 1825-1856.
II. Title. III. Series.
PN1040.A513   1992
808.2—dc20   92-33258
                                                                    CIP

Printed in Canada on acid-free paper.

ARISTOTLE was born in 384 B.C. in the Northern Greek town of Stagira, where his father was the personal physician to the great-grandfather of Alexander the Great. At the age of eighteen Aristotle entered Plato's Academy and soon became recognized as its most important student. He remained under Plato's tutelage for nearly twenty years.

After his teacher's death in 347 B.C., Aristotle cultivated associations with other Academy students throughout Greece and Asia Minor. Then in 342 B.C., Aristotle was asked by King Philip II of Macedonia to become the tutor for his young son Alexander, who was later to become the conqueror of much of the known world at that time. The young prince remained under Aristotle's supervision until 336 B.C., when he acceded to the throne after his father's death. Two years later, Aristotle returned to Athens and founded his own school, which he called the Lyceum. This intellectual center flourished during the years when Alexander the Great ruled Greece as part of his large empire. But upon Alexander's death in 323 B.C., Aristotle was charged with impiety by Athenians who resented his associations with the Macedonian conqueror. Rather than risk the same fate as Plato's mentor Socrates, Aristotle fled to the city of Chalcis, where he died in 322 B.C.

Aristotle's interests, like those of Plato, were diverse and his writing cast its shadow on many fields, including logic, metaphysics, esthetics, epistemology, ethics, politics, and the sciences. Among his most well-known works are: *The Categories, The Prior and Posterior Analytics, The Physics, The Metaphysics, De Anima, The Nicomachean Ethics, Poetics,* and *The Politics.*

Series Editor's Foreword

In his notes to the *Poetics,* Buckley refers to a number of previous editions, translations, and commentaries on this work. The most prominent are given below:

Dacier, tr. and comm. *La Poétique d'Aristote, contenant les règles les plus exactes pour juger du Poème Heroïque, et des Pièces de Théâtre, la Tragédie et la Comédie.* Amsterdam: Covens et Mortier, 1733.

Ritter, Francis. *Poetica. Ad codices antiquos recognitam, latine conversam, commentario illustratam edidit Franciscus Ritter.* Cologne: C. Baedeker, 1839.

Taylor, Thomas, trans. *The Rhetoric, Poetic, and Nicomachean Ethics of Aristotle.* 2 vols. London, 1818.

Twining, Thomas. *Treatise on Poetry, translated with notes on the translation and on the Original and two dissertations on poetical and musical imitation.* London: Payne and Son, 1789.

Additional Notes:

P. 7, n. 3:
From the *Margites*:
The gods made him neither a digger nor a plougher nor skilled in any other handicraft: he missed the mark in all.
"And again,
'He knew many things, but he knew nothing w ⁻ⁱⁱ.' "

P. 39, n. 6:

Horace, *Ars Poetica* (*The Art of Poetry*):
The chorus should sustain the part and strenuous duty of actor, nor should there be a choral entr'acte that does not advance and fit appropriately into the plot.

P. 41, n. 1:

Quintilian, *Institutio Oratoria* (*The Principles of Rhetoric*):
The same circumstance admits all the figures of sense . . . into which many have divided the types of speeches. For we ask questions, express doubts, affirm, threaten, and pray.

P. 49:

". . . making Iambics even in common discourse; as 'Verily I saw the Grace Marathonward walking.'
And,
'At least he would not long for that hellbore.' "
[It is impossible, given the context, to determine exactly the meaning of the last line. The point here is that Euclides is parodying Homer's occasional irrational lengthening of short syllables.]

P. 50:

"But Euripides . . . And,
'Being little and worthless and feeble,'
by inserting proper [and common] words, it will be,
'Being small and weak and hideous.'
And,
'Putting down a shabby chair and a small table.'
'Putting down a poor chair and a little table.' "

P. 51, n. 12:
Rhetoric 3. 11. 5:
It is the privilege of one who conjectures happily, to discern the point of similitude. (tr. T. Buckley).

P. 61:
"And at the same time he says:
'When he looked toward the plain of Troy, he marveled at the din of flutes and pipes. . . .'
And thus, 'It alone has no share. . . .'
. . . as Hippias the Thasian solved the following passages: 'We grant to him [the fulfillment of his prayer].' "

P. 62, n. 18:
Scholiast's note to *Iliad,* Book 19, v. 238: The ancient custom was to call iron bronze; of course, iron workers are braziers.

THE POETIC.

CHAP. I.

*On Poetry in general, as an imitative Art, and its different
Species.*

LET us speak concerning poetry itself, and its [dif- 1. On Po-
ferent] species[1]; what power each possesses, and how etry, its
influence
fables must be composed, in order that poetry may and spe-
be such as is fitting: further still, [let us show] of cies.
how many and what kind of parts it consists; and
in like manner [let us treat] concerning such other
things as pertain to this method, beginning, con-
formably to nature, first from such things as are
first.

The epopee, therefore, and tragic poetry, and 2. The
moreover comedy, and dithyrambic poetry, and the imitative
arts.
greatest part of the art pertaining to the flute and
the lyre[2], are all entirely imitations[3]. They differ, 3. Their
however, in three things; for [they differ] either by differ-
imitating through means different in kind, or by imi- ence.
tating different objects, or in a different, and not after
the same manner. For as certain persons assimi- 4.
lating, imitate many things by colours and figures,
some indeed through art, but others through custom,
[and others through voice][4]; thus also in the afore-

---

[1] "Poesis in *species* sive *formas* (εἶδη), formæ rursus in
partes (μόρια, μέρη) dividuntur." Ritter.
[2] Cf. Plato Theag. p. 10. C. Cithern-playing was one of the
favourite accomplishments of the Athenian youth, ibid. p. 8. E.
Alcib. Pr. p. 26. D. Læm. and Olympiodor. in eund. t. ii. p.
65. ed. Creuz.
[3] See Ritter, and Twining's Dissertations and first note.
[4] Hermann reads φύσεως for φωνῆς with Madius, but Ritter
condemns the words as spurious.

mentioned arts, all of them indeed produce imitation in rhythm, words, and harmony ; and in these, either distinctly, or mingled together, as, for instance, the arts of the flute and the lyre alone employ harmony and rhythm[5] ; and this will also be the case with any other arts which possess a power of this kind, such as the art of playing on reed-pipes. But the arts pertaining to dancing imitate by rhythm, without harmony ; for dancers, through figured rhythms, imitate manners, and passions, and actions. But the epopee alone imitates by mere words[6] or metres, and by these either mingling them with each other, or employing one certain kind of metres, which method has been adopted up to the present time[7]. For otherwise we should have no common name, by which we could denominate the Mimes of Sophron and Xenarchus, and the dialogues of Socrates; or those who imitate by trimetres, or elegies, or certain other things of this kind ; except that men joining with metre the verb *to make*[8], call some of these *makers of elegies*, but others epic *makers*, not as poets according to imi-

5.
Dancing imitates by rhythm only.
6. The epopee by words.
7. Etymology of the name Poet.

---

[5] Cf. Rhet. iii. 8.

[6] There is much difficulty about this definition of ἐποποιία, as λόγοις ψιλοῖς is supposed by some to mean *prose*, (see Robortell. p. 14,) by others, *verse without music*. The former opinion is advocated by Hermann, the latter by Buhle. Ritter seems to have clearly shown that ἢ τοῖς μέτροις is added, not as an explanation of λόγοις ψιλοῖς, but disjunctively, and that ἐποποιία is used in a new sense for certain parts of prose-writing as well as verse. The sense is, therefore, " by prose or by metre, but unaccompanied by song."

[7] Ritter observes that the following passage is an excuse for the new signification of ἐποποιία.

[8] It may be necessary to observe, that the Greek word (ποιητης—*poiétes*) whence *poeta*, and *poet*, is, literally, *maker ;* and maker, it is well known, was once the current term for *poet* in our language ; and to write verses, was, to *make*. Sir Philip Sidney, speaking of the Greek word, says, " wherein, I know not whether by luck or wisdom, we Englishmen have *met* with the Greeks, in calling him *maker*." Defense of Poesy.

So Spenser :

The god of shepherds, *Tityrus*, is dead,
Who taught me, homely, as I can, to MAKE.
          Shep. Cal. June.   Twining.

tation, but denominating them in common according to measure. For they are accustomed thus to denominate them, if they write any thing medical or musical in verse. There is, however, nothing common to Homer and Empedocles except the measure; on which account, it is right indeed to call the former a poet; but the latter, a physiologist rather than a poet. In like manner, though some one, mingling all the measures, should produce imitation, as Chære-mon has done in his *Centaur*, a mixed rhapsody of all the metres, yet he must not be called a poet[9]. Let it then be thus laid down concerning these particulars. But there are some kinds of poetry which employ all the before-mentioned means, I mean, rhythm, melody, and measure, such as dithyrambic poetry and the Nomes[10], and also tragedy and comedy. But these differ, because some of them use all these at once, but others partially. I speak, therefore, of these differences of the arts in respect to the means by which they produce imitation.

8. Which name is common to writers on other subjects.

9. But the adherence to metre does not make the poet.

10. Means respectively employed by the different kinds of poetry.

CHAP. II.

On Imitation, and its usual Objects.

BUT since imitators imitate those who do something, and it is necessary that these should either be worthy or depraved persons; (for manners nearly always depend on these alone, since all men differ in their manners by vice and virtue;) it is necessary either [to imitate] those who are better than we are,

1. Objects of imitation either good or bad, as in painting.

---

9 "For imitation makes the poet, not the metre." Ritter.

10 In dithyrambic or *Bacchic* hymns, and in the *Nomes*, which were also a species of hymns to Apollo and other deities, *all* the means of imitation were employed *together*, and *throughout*: in tragedy and comedy, *separately*; some of them in one part of the drama, and some in another. In the *choral* part, however, at least, if no where else, *all*, melody, rhythm, and words, must probably have been used *at once*, as in the hymns. Twining.

or those who are worse, or such as are like ourselves [1], in the same manner as painters do. For Polygnotus, indeed, painted men more beautiful than they are, but Pauson less so, and Dionysius painted them as
2. And they are [2]. But it is evident that each of the before-
imitations
different. mentioned imitations will have these differences ; and imitation is different, by imitating different things
3. after this manner. For there may be differences of this kind in dancing, in playing on the flute, on the lyre, and also in orations and mere measure. Thus Homer imitates better men [3] [than exist], but Cleophon men as they are; and Hegemon the Thasian, who first made parodies, and Nicochares, who wrote
4. the Deliad, imitate worse characters. In like manner in dithyrambics and the Nomi, [as Timotheus and Philoxenus have imitated the Persians and the Cyclops,] one may imitate [4]. By this very same difference, also, tragedy differs from comedy. For the one seeks to imitate worse, but the other better men than are.

CHAP. III.

The third difference of Poetry according to the manner of imitating.

1. Imita-
tions dif- THERE is also a third difference of these, consist-
ferent in ing in the manner in which one may imitate each of
the man-
ner.

[1] Or, "those who are commonly found."

[2] Polygnotus and Dionysius lived about Ol. 80; Pauson about Ol. 90. On the following poets see Ritter.

[3] Superior, that is, in courage, strength, wisdom, prudence, etc.—in *any* laudable, useful, or admirable quality, whether such as we denominate *moral*, or not. If superiority of *moral* character only were meant, the assertion would be false.—It is necessary to remember here, the *wide* sense in which the ancients used the terms *virtue, vice—good, bad*, etc. See note 19.—The difference between *moral* and *poetical* perfection of character, is well explained by Dr. Beattie, *Essay on Poetry*, etc., Part I. ch. 4. The heroes of Homer, as he well observes, are "*finer animals*" than we are, (p. 69,) not *better men*. Twining.

[4] Ritter would throw out the words enclosed in brackets. See his note.

them. For by the same instruments the same things may be imitated, the poet sometimes himself narrating, and sometimes assuming another person [as Homer does][1] ; or speaking as the same person without any change; or as all imitate [who do so] by deed and action. But imitation consists in these three differences, as we said in the beginning; viz. in the means, the objects, or the manner. Hence, Sophocles will in one respect be the same imitator as Homer, for both of them imitate elevated characters; and in another the same as Aristophanes, for both of them imitate persons engaged in acting; [[2]whence also it is said that certain persons call their works *dramas*, because they imitate those who are engaged in *doing* something. On this account the Dorians lay claim to the invention of tragedy and comedy; of comedy indeed the Megarians, as well those who are natives of Greece, as being invented by them at the time when their government was a democracy, as those of Sicily. For thence was the poet Epicharmus, who was much prior to Chonides and Magnes. But some of those Dorians who inhabit Peloponnesus lay claim to tragedy, making names an evidence. For they allege that they call their villages *komai*, but the Athenians *demoi ;* as if comedians were not so denominated from *komazein*, [i. e. *to revel*,] but from their wandering through villages, being ignominiously expelled from the cities. The verb *poiein* also, or *to make*, is by the Dorians denominated *dran*, but by the Athenians *prattein*.]
And thus much concerning the differences of imitation, as to their number and quality.

2. And the differences of imitation are three.

3. Etymology of the drama andclaims to its invention.

4.

---

[1] But this assertion is not correct, and Ritter shows that the words are spurious.

[2] The learned note of Ritter seems to condemn the whole of this passage as spurious.

CHAP. IV.

The Causes and Progress of Poetry.

1. Two causes
2. of poetry, and those natural: the first, the natural taste for imitation,
3. seen in respect to the works of art;
4. because to learn is ever pleasant.
5. Hence a delight in images.

TWO causes, however, and these physical, appear to have produced poetry in general. For to imitate is congenial to men from childhood. And in this they differ from other animals, that they are most imitative, and acquire the first disciplines through imitation; and that all men delight in imitations. But an evidence of this is that which happens in the works [of artists]. For we are delighted on surveying very accurate images, the realities of which are painful to the view; such as the forms of the most contemptible animals, and dead bodies. The cause, however, of this is, that learning is not only most delightful to philosophers, but in like manner to other persons, though they partake of it but in a small degree. For on this account, men are delighted on surveying images, because it happens that by surveying they learn and infer what each particular is; as, that *this* is an image of *that man;* since, unless one happen to have seen [the reality], it is not the imitation that pleases [1], but [it is through] either the workmanship, or the colour, or some other cause of

6. And from imitation, harmony, and rhythm,

the like kind. But imitation, harmony, and rhythm being natural to us, (for it is evident that measures or metres are parts of rhythms,[2]) the earliest among mankind, making a gradual progress in these things

---

[1] Ritter well reads οὐχὶ μίμημα ἢ μίμημα.

[2] "RHYTHM differs from METRE, inasmuch as RHYTHM is *proportion, applied to any motion whatever;* METRE is *proportion, applied to the motion of* WORDS SPOKEN. Thus, in the drumming of a march, or the dancing of a hornpipe, there is *rhythm,* though *no metre;* in *Dryden's* celebrated Ode there is METRE as well as RHYTHM, because the poet with the *rhythm* has associated certain *words.* And hence it follows, that, though ALL METRE is RHYTHM, yet ALL RHYTHM is NOT METRE." Harris's Philol. Inquiries, p. 67,—where it is also observed, very truly, that "no English word expresses *rhythmus* better than the word *time.*" P. 69, note. Twining.

from the beginning, produced poetry from extempo- men ori-
raneous efforts. But poetry was divided according ginally produced
to appropriate manners. For men of a more vener- poetry,
able character imitated beautiful actions, and the 7. which
actions of such men; but the more ignoble imitated was va-
ried ac-
the actions of depraved characters, first composing cording to
vituperative verses, in the same manner as the others suitable
manners.
composed hymns and encomiums. Of the authors,
therefore, before Homer, we cannot mention any poem 8. No sati-
of this kind; though it is probable that there were rical poe-
try before
many such writers. But if we begin from Homer, Homer's
there are such for instance as his Margites[3], and some Margites.
others, in which, as being suited, the measure is
Iambic. Hence, also, the Iambic verse is now called,
because in this metre they used to *Iambize* (i. e. de-
fame) each other. Of ancient poets, likewise, some 9. The old
composed heroic poems, and others Iambic. But as poets
thence
Homer was the greatest of poets on serious subjects, were ei-
(and this not only because he alone imitated well, but ther hero-
also because he made dramatic imitations,) thus too ic or Iam-
bic.
he first demonstrated the figures of comedy, not dra-
matically exhibiting invective, but ridicule. For the
Margites bears the same analogy to comedy, as the
Iliad and Odyssey to tragedy. But when tragedy 10. Pro-
and comedy had appeared, those poets who were na- gress of
turally impelled to each kind of poetry, some, instead the two
styles,
of writing Iambics, became comic poets, but others, upon the
instead of [writing] epic poems, became the authors introduc-
tion of
of tragedies, because these forms [of poetry] are tragedy
greater and more esteemed than those. To con- and
sider, therefore, whether tragedy is now perfect comedy.
11.
in its species or not, regarded as well with reference to itself as to the theatres, is the business of 12. Both
another treatise. Both tragedy and comedy, there- at first ex-
tempora-
fore, at first originated from extemporaneous efforts. neous.

---

[3] The character of the hero is handed down to us thus :

Τὸν δ' οὔτ' ἀρ σκαπτῆρα θεοὶ θέσαν οὔτ' ἀροτῆρα
οὔτ' ἄλλως τε σοφόν, πάσης δ' ἡμάρτανε τέχνης.

And again,

πολλ' ἠπίστατο ἔργα, κακῶς δ' ἠπίστατο πάντα.

A character not unlike Sir Abel Handy in Morton's " School
of Reform."

And tragedy, indeed, originated from those who led the dithyramb, but comedy from those who sung the Phallic verses, which even now in many cities remain in use; and it gradually increased as obvious improvements became known. And tragedy, having experienced many changes, rested when it had arrived at its proper nature. Æschylus, also, first increased the number of players from one to two[4], abridged the functions of the chorus, and made one of the players act the chief part[5]. But Sophocles introduced three players into the scene, and added scenic painting. Further still, the magnitude [of tragedy increased] from small fables and ridiculous diction, in consequence of having been changed from satyric[6] composition, it was late before it acquired dignity. The metre also of tragedy, from tetrameter, became Iambic (for at first they used tetrameter in tragedy, because poetry was then satyrical, and more adapted to the dance, but dialogue being adopted, nature herself discovered a suitable metre; for the Iambic measure is most of all adapted to conversation. And as an evidence of this, we most frequently speak in Iambics in familiar discourse with each other; but we seldom speak in hexameters, and then only when we depart from that harmony which is adapted to conversation). Again, tragedy is said to have been further adorned, with a multitude of episodes, and other particulars. Let, therefore, thus much said suffice concerning these things; for it would perhaps be a great toil to discuss every particular.

13. Æschylus improves tragedy, and then Sophocles.

14. It becomes elevated in style.

Suitableness of the Iambic metre.

15.

[4] See my introduction to Æschylus, p. vii. ed. Bohn.

[5] See ibid. note.

[6] *Satyric*, from the share which those fantastic beings called *Satyrs*, the companions and *play-fellows* of *Bacchus*, had in the earliest Tragedy, of which they formed the chorus. *Joking* and *dancing* were essential attributes of these rustic semi-deities. Hence the "*ludicrous language*" and the "*dancing genius*" of the old Tragedy, to which the TROCHAIC or *running* metre here spoken of was peculiarly adapted; being no other than this:

"Jolly mortals, fill your glasses, noble deeds are done by wine."

The reader will not confound *satyric* with *satiric;* nor the

CHAP. V.

On Comedy, and its Origin.—Difference of Epopee and Tragedy.

BUT comedy is, as we have said, an imitation indeed of bad characters, yet it does not imitate them according to every vice, [but the ridiculous only;] since the ridiculous is a portion of turpitude. For *the ridiculous is a certain error, and turpitude unattended with pain, and not destructive.* Thus, for instance, a ridiculous face is something deformed and distorted without pain. The transitions, therefore, of tragedy, and the causes through which they are produced, are not unknown; but [those of] comedy have escaped our knowledge, because it was not at first an object of attention. For it was late before the magistrate gave a chorus to comedians[1]; but prior to that period, the choruses were voluntary. Comedy, however, at length having obtained a certain form, those who are said to have been poets therein are commemorated. But it is unknown who it was that introduced masks or prologues,[2] or a multitude of players, and such like particulars. But Epicharmus and Phormis [were the first] to compose fables; which, therefore, originated from Sicily. But among the Athenians, Crates, rejecting the Iambic[3]

1. Comedy an imitation of the ridiculous.

2. Its changes not known.

3. Nor the inventors of masks, etc.

Greek *satyric* drama with the *satire* of Roman origin. See Harris's Phil. Arrang. p. 460, note. Dacier's Preface to Horace's Satires. The two words are of different derivations. Twining.

[1] This was almost equivalent to the modern "licensing" of plays, but was probably conducted with more taste and less absurdity. The poet was said αἰτεῖν χορόν, the choragus διδόναι, and, if the piece was approved by the archon, the poet χορὸν ἔλαβε. See Ritter.

[2] But this is evidently corrupt. Ritter reads λόγους with Hermann, understanding those passages which the single actor either recited, or spoke in conversation with the chorus, opposing λόγοι ὑποκριτῶν to the ἄσματα κωμῳδῶν.

[3] *Iambic,* i. e. *satirical,* and *personally* so, like the old *Iambi,*

form, first began generally to compose speeches and

4. Similarity of tragedy to epic poetry. fables. The epopee, therefore, is an attendant on tragedy, [with the exception of the long metre[4],] since through this it is an imitation of worthy characters and actions. But it differs from tragedy in that it has a simple metre, and is a narration. It also [differs from it] in length. For tragedy is especially limited by one period of the sun, or admits but a small variation from this period; but the epopee is not defined within a certain time, and in this it differs; though at first they observed the same conduct with tragedy[5], no less than epic po-

5. Their common and distinctive parts. etry. With respect to the parts, however, [of the epopee and tragedy,] some are the same in both, but others are peculiar to tragedy. Hence he who knows what is a good or bad tragedy, knows the same in respect to epic poetry. For those things which the epopee possesses are to be found in tragedy; but every thing which tragedy contains is not in the epopee.

CHAP. VI.

On the Form and End of Tragedy, and on its six parts,
especially the Plot.

1. CONCERNING, therefore, imitative poetry in hexameters, and comedy, we shall speak hereafter. Let us now, however, speak concerning tragedy, assuming the definition of its essence as arising from what has **2. Definition of tragedy.** been already said. *Tragedy, therefore, is an imitation of a worthy or illustrious and perfect action,*

invectives, or lampoons, of which Aristotle speaks above, and from which the *Iambic metre,* which is not here alluded to, took its name. Twining.

[4] The words μέχρι μόνου μέτρου μεγάλου or μετὰ λόγου are thrown out by Ritter, and can have no meaning.

[5] On the question of the unities, see Twining, note 43, and my own note on Æsch. Eum. 235.

*possessing magnitude, in pleasing language, using
separately the several species of imitation in its parts,
by men acting, and not through narration, through
pity and fear effecting a purification from such like
passions*[1]. But by *pleasing language*, I mean language possessing rhythm, harmony, and melody.
And it *uses separately the several species* [*of imitation*], because some parts of the tragedy are alone
perfected through metres, and others again through
melody. But since they produce imitation by acting, in the first place the ornament of the spectacle[2]
will be a certain part of the tragedy, and in the next
place the melopœia[3] and the diction. For by these
they produce imitation. But I call diction, indeed,
the composition of the metres; and melopœia that,
the whole power of which is apparent. Since, however, [tragedy] is an imitation of action, and action
is effected by certain agents, who must needs be persons of a certain description both as to their manners
and their sentiments[4], (for from these we say that

3. Its language, and different manners of imitation: 4. of scenery, melopœia, and diction.

5. Two causes of action, sentiments, and moral habit.

---

[1] On the different interpretations of this difficult passage,
see Twining, note 45. Ritter has followed the views of Lessing, in a note too full of argument to admit of condensation.
Taylor's note is, as usual, a blundering Neo-Platonic attempt
to reconcile the discrepancies of Aristotle and Plato.

[2] *Decoration*—literally, the decoration of the *spectacle*, or
sight. In other places it is called the *spectacle*, or *sight* only
—ὄψις. It comprehends *scenery*, *dresses*—the whole visible
apparatus of the theatre. I do not know any single English
word that answers fully to the Greek word. Twining.

[3] *Melopœia*—literally, the *making*, or the *composition, of the
Music*; as we use *Epopœia*, or according to the French termination, which we have naturalized, *Epopee*, to signify epic *poetry*,
or *epic-making*, in general.—I might have rendered it, at once,
the MUSIC; but that it would have appeared ridiculous to observe, of a word so familiar to us, even that "*its meaning is
obvious*." Twining.

[4] *Dianoia*—διανοία, in a general way, may be defined to be
διεξοδικὴ τοῦ λόγου ἐνεργεία, i. e. *the discursive energy of reason*. But accurately speaking, it is *that power of soul which
reasons scientifically, deriving the principles of its reasoning from
intellect*. This latter definition, however, pertains to it, so far
as it is not influenced in its reasonings by imagination and false
opinions. TAYLOR, who objects to translating it "sentiments."
I prefer following Twining, understanding sentiments not ex-

actions derive their quality,) hence there are naturally two causes of actions, sentiments and moral habit, and through these actions all men obtain or fail of

6. Definition of fable, manners, and sentiment.

the object of their wishes. But a fable, indeed, is an imitation of action; for I mean by a *fable* here, the composition of incidents. By *manners*, I mean those things according to which we say that agents are persons of a certain character; and by *sentiment*, that through which those who speak demonstrate any thing, or explain their meaning. It is necessary,

7. Six parts in every tragedy.

therefore, that the parts of every tragedy should be six, from which the tragedy derives its quality. But these are, fable and manners, diction and sentiment, spectacle and melopœia. Of these parts, however, two pertain to the means by which they imitate; one, to the manner; and three, to the objects[5]. And be-

8. Some tragic poets use all these parts.

sides these, there are no other. [Not a few [tragic poets], therefore, as I may say, use all these parts[6].] For every tragedy has scenic apparatus, manners, and a fable, and melody, and, in a similar manner, sentiment. But the greatest of these is the combina-

9. Tragedy an imitation of actions.

tion of the incidents. For tragedy is an imitation not of men, but of actions, [of life, and of felicity. For infelicity consists in action, and the end is a certain

10. What constitutes character. Manner not the end of tragedy; 11. but action.

action, and not a quality[7].] Men, however, are persons of a certain character, according to their manners; but according to their actions, they are happy, or the contrary. The end of tragedy, therefore, does not consist in imitating manners, but it embraces manners on account of actions; so that the action and the fable are the end of tragedy. But the end is the greatest of all things. Moreover, without action, tragedy cannot exist; but it may exist without

pressed, (γνώμαι, cf. Rhet. ii. 21,) but in the mind, and forming the mainspring of action.

[5] i. e. λέξις and μελοποιία are the means or instruments, ὄψις the manner, μῦθος, ἤθη, and διανοία, the objects.

[6] An evident interpolation. See Ritter.

[7] Thus stands the text, as freed from the additions made by Aldus, or other Italian critics. But the whole passage is probably an interpolation, as Ritter seems to have clearly shown. See his judicious note.

manners. For most modern tragedies are without
manners; and in short, many poets are such as
among painters Zeuxis is when compared with Polygnotus. For Polygnotus, indeed, painted the manners of the good; but the pictures of Zeuxis are
without manners. Further still, if any one place in 12. Proof.
a continued series moral speeches, sayings, and sentiments well framed, he will not produce that which is
the work of tragedy; but that will be much more a
tragedy, which uses these things as subordinate, and
which contains a fable and combination of incidents.
Add to this, that the greatest parts by which fable 13. The
allures the soul, are the *revolutions* and *discoveries*. revolu-
Again, it is likewise an evidence of this, that those discovery
who attempt to write tragedies, acquire the power of cause
expressing a thing in tragic diction and manners ac- most plea-
curately, before they can compose a fable, as was the 14. Proof
case with nearly all the first poets. The fable, there- from the
fore, is the principal part, and as it were the soul of of forming
tragedy; but the manners are next in rank [8]. [Just as 15. Com-
in painting, if any one were to spread the most beauti- parison of
ful pigments on promiscuously, he would not please painting.
the view so much as by outlining an image with white
colour only. Tragedy also is an imitation of action,
and on this account, especially, [an imitation] of
agents. But the sentiments rank third. And by them 16. Defi-
[I mean] *the power of explaining what is inherent* nition of
in the subject, and adapted to it, which is the pecu- ment.
liar province of politics [9] and rhetoric. For the ancient poets represent those whom they introduce as
speaking politically; but those of the present day,
rhetorically. But the manners are, whatever shows 17. Of
what the deliberate choice is. Hence those speeches manners
are without manners, in which there is altogether sentiment.

[8] The rest of this chapter is condemned by Ritter as an interpolation.
[9] The reader, here, must not think of our modern *politics.*
—The *political,* or *civil art,* or *science,* was, in Aristotle's view,
of wide extent and high importance. It comprehended *ethics*
and *eloquence,* or the art of public speaking; every thing, in
short, that concerned the well-being of a *state.*—See note 57.
Twining.

nothing that the speaker may choose or avoid[10]. But *sentiment is that through which they show that a certain thing is, or is not, or by which they universally enunciate something.* And the fourth part of tragedy is diction. But I say, as was before observed, that *diction is interpretation by the means of words, and which also has the same power in verse and prose.* But of the remaining five, the melopœia is the greatest of the embellishments. But the scenic decoration is alluring indeed; yet it is most inartificial, and is in the smallest degree akin to poetry. For the power of tragedy remains, even when unaccompanied with scenic apparatus and players. And further still, the art of the mechanic possesses more power in constructing the scenic apparatus than that of the poet.]

18. Of diction.

19. Melopœia and spectacle, the latter least pertaining to art.

CHAP. VII.

On the Requisites and Length of Tragic Action.

1. Definition of a plot.

THESE things being defined, let us in the next place show what the combination of the incidents ought to be, since this is the first and greatest part of tragedy.

2. But it is granted to us, that tragedy is the imitation of a perfect and whole action, and of one which possesses a certain magnitude; for there may be a whole which has no magnitude. But a whole is that which has a beginning, middle, and end. And the beginning is that which necessarily is not itself posterior to another thing; but another thing is naturally expected to follow it. On the contrary, the end is that which is itself naturally adapted to be posterior to another thing, either from necessity, or for the most part; but after this there is nothing else. But the middle is that which is itself after another thing, and after which there is something else. Hence, it is necessary that those who compose fables properly, should neither

3. Of a dramatic whole, and its parts.

[10] These words are differently placed in some editions.

begin them casually, nor end them casually, but should employ the above-mentioned forms [of beginning, middle, and end]. Further still, since that which is beautiful, whether it be an animal, or any thing else which is composed from certain parts, ought not only to have these parts arranged, but a magnitude also which is not casual. For the beautiful consists in magnitude and order. Hence, neither can any very small animal be beautiful; for the survey of it is confused, since it is effected in a time nearly insensible. Nor yet a very large animal; for it is not surveyed at once, but its subsistence as one and a whole escapes the view of the spectators; such as if, for instance, it should be an animal of ten thousand stadia in length. Hence, as in bodies and in animals it is necessary there should be magnitude; but such as can easily be seen; thus also in fables, there should be length, but this such as can easily be remembered[1]. The definition, however, of the length with reference to contests[2] and the senses, does not fall under the consideration of art. For if it were requisite to perform a hundred tragedies, [as is said to have been the case more than once[3],] the performance ought to be regulated by a clepsydra. But the definition [of the length of the fable] according to the nature of the thing, is this, that the fable is always more beautiful the greater it is, if at the same time it is perspicuous. Simply defining the thing, however, we may say, [that a fable has an appropriate magnitude,] when the time of its duration is such as to render it probable that there can be a transition from prosperous to adverse, or from adverse to prosperous fortune, according to the necessary or probable order

4. Magnitude and order the constituents of beauty.

5. Magnitude in reference to plots;

6. 1stly, as to dramatic exhibitions.

7. 2ndly, as to intrinsic value.

---

[1] The unity here spoken of, it must be remembered, is not *absolute* and *simple*, but *relative* and *compound*, unity; a unity consisting of different *parts*, the relation of which to each other, and to the whole, is easily perceived at one view. On this depends the perception of beauty in *form*.—In objects too extended, you may be said to have *parts*, but no *whole*: in very minute objects the *whole*, but no *parts*. Twining.

[2] i. e. to its representation at the dramatic contests.

[3] These words are condemned by Ritter.

of things as they take place. This is a sufficient
definition of magnitude.

CHAP. VIII.

On the Unity of the Fable.

1. On
dramatic
unity.

THE fable, however, is one, not as some suppose, if
one person is the subject of it; for many things
which are infinite in kind happen [to one man],
from a certain number of which no one event arises.
Thus, also, there are many actions of one man, from

2. Previous mis-
concep-
tions on
the sub-
ject.
3. Con-
duct of
Homer.

which no one action is produced. Hence all those
poets appear to have erred who have written the
Heracleid, and Theseid, and such like poems. For
they suppose that because Hercules was one person,
it was fit that the fable should be one. Homer, however, as he excelled in other things, appears likewise
to have seen this clearly, whether from art, or from
nature. For in composing the Odyssey, he has not
related every thing which happened to Ulysses; such
as the being wounded in Parnassus[1], and pretending
to be insane[2] at the muster of the Greeks; one of
which taking place, it was not necessary or probable
that the other should happen; but he composed the

4. Appli-
cation of
unity to
the plot.

Odyssey, as also his Iliad, upon one[3] action. It is
requisite, therefore, that as in other imitative arts
one imitation[4] is the imitation of one thing, thus,

---

[1] *This* incident is, however, related, and at considerable
length, in the xixth book of the Odyssey, (v. 563 of Pope's
translation,) but digressively, and incidentally; it made no
essential part of his *general plan.* Twining.

[2] A ridiculous story.—"To avoid going to the Trojan war,
Ulysses pretended to be mad; and, to prove his insanity, went
to plough with an *ox* and a *horse;* but Palamedes, in order to
detect him, laid his infant son, Telemachus, in the way of the
plough; upon which Ulysses immediately stopped, and there-
by proved himself to be in his right senses."—(Hyginus, etc.)
Twining.

[3] I follow Ritter's text.

[4] i. e. one *imitative work.* Thus *one* picture represents, or

also, [in tragedy,] the fable, since it is an imitation
of action, should be the imitation of one action, and
of the whole of this, and that the parts of the transactions should be so arranged, that any one of them
being transposed, or taken away, the whole would
become different and changed. For that which
when present or not present produces no sensible
[difference], is not a part of the fable[5].

CHAP. IX.

*On the difference between History and Poetry, and how his-
torical matter should be used in Poetry.*

BUT it is evident from what has been said, that it is
not the province of a poet to relate things which
have happened, but such as might have happened,
and such things as are possible according to probability, or which would necessarily have happened[1].
For an historian and a poet do not differ from each
other, because the one writes in verse and the other
in prose; for the history of Herodotus might be
written in verse, and yet it would be no less a history

1. The poet does not relate real events,

2. for then he would clash with the histo-rian.

should represent, but *one* thing;—a single *object*, or a single
action, etc. So, every poem (the *Orlando Furioso* as much as
the *Iliad*) is *one imitation*—one imitative *work*, and should
imitate *one* action, in Aristotle's sense of *unity*, like the poems
of Homer; not a number of actions unconnected with each
other, or connected merely by their common *relation* to *one*
person, as in the *Theseids*, etc., or to one *time*, as in the poem
of Ariosto; or, by their *resemblance* merely, as in the *Me-
tamorphoses* of *Ovid.* Twining.

[5] "The *painter* will not inquire what things may be admitted without much censure. He will not think it enough to
show that they *may* be there, he will show that they *must* be
there; that their *absence* would render his picture *maimed* and
defective.—They should make *a part of that whole which would
be imperfect without them.*"—Sir J. Reynolds, Disc. on Painting, p. 106. Twining.

[1] Cf. Sheridan's Critic, vii. 1. "What the plague! a play
is not to show occurrences that happen every day, but things
just so strange, that though they never did, they might happen."

with metre, than without metre. But they differ in this, that the one speaks of things which have happened, and the other of such as might have happened.

3. Hence poetry is universal and philosophic.

Hence, poetry is more philosophic, and more deserving of attention, than history. For poetry speaks more of universals, but history of particulars. But

4. Definition of universal and particular.

universal consists indeed in relating or performing certain things which happen to a man of a certain description, either probably or necessarily, [to which the aim of poetry is directed in giving names[2];] but *particular* consists in narrating what, [for example,]

5. As is evident in comedy.

Alcibiades did, or what he suffered. In comedy, therefore, this is now become evident. For [comic poets] having composed a fable through things of a probable nature, they thus give whatever names they please[3] to their characters, and do not, like Iambic poets, write poems about particular persons. But in

6. Real names retained in tragedy,

tragedy they cling to real names. The cause, however, of this is that the possible is credible. Things, therefore, which have not yet been done, we do not yet believe to be possible; but it is evident that things which have been done are possible; for they would not have been done, if they were impossible.

7. but not real names only.

Not, indeed, but that in some tragedies there are one or two of known names, and the rest are feigned; but in others there is no known name; as, for instance, in *the Flower* of Agatho. For in this tragedy, the things and the names are alike feigned, and yet it

8. Nor must we entirely confine ourselves to traditional fables.

delights no less. Hence, one must not seek to adhere entirely to traditional fables, which are the subjects of tragedy. For it is ridiculous to make this the object of search, because even known subjects are known but to a few, though at the same time they

---

[2] Ritter well observes that the perspicuity of this otherwise clear passage is destroyed by this absurd interpolation.

[3] Thus nearly all the names in the tragedies of Terence and Plautus, thus Dromo and Sosia are applied to slaves, Pamphilus to a lover, Glycerium or Philumena to a lady, Pyrgopolinices or Thraso to soldiers. Also the names in Petronius and Apuleius, as Pannychis, Meroe, Fotis, etc. So Ben Jonson has personified the virtues and vices in "Cynthia's Revels," and elsewhere.

delight all men. From these things, therefore, it is evident that a poet ought rather to be the author of fables than of metres, inasmuch as he is a poet from imitation, and he imitates actions. Hence, though it should happen that he relates things which have happened, he is no less a poet. For nothing hinders but that some actions which have happened, are such as might both probably[4] and possibly have happened, and by [the narration of] such he is a poet.

But of simple plots and actions, the episodic are the worst. But I call the plot episodic, in which it is neither probable nor necessary that the episodes follow each other. Such plots, however, are com-

9. Hence the plot, rather than the metre, is the poet's object.

10. Objection to, and definition of, episodic fables.

[4] It may appear to the reader to be a strange observation, that "*some true* events MAY be *probable*." But he will recollect what sort of *events*, and what sort of *probability*, Aristotle here speaks of: i. e. of *extraordinary events*, such as Poetry requires, and of that more *strict* and *perfect probability*, that closer connexion and *visible* dependence of circumstances, which are always required from the *poet*, though in *such* events, not often to be found in *fact*, and real life, and therefore not expected from the *historian*.

Aristotle alludes to these two lines of Agatho :

Τάχ' ἄν τις εἰκὸς αὐτὸ τῦτ' εἶναι λέγοι,
Βροτοῖσι πολλὰ τυγχάνειν ἐκ εἰκότα.

Even *this*, it may be said, is *probable*,
That many things *improbable* should happen,
In human life.—

See Rhet. ii. 24. 10, and Bayle's Dict. Art. AGATHON, note [F], who mentions a similar maxim of St. Bernard's : "Ordinatissimum est, minus interdum ordinatè fieri." "Il est tout à fait de l'ordre, que de tems en tems il se fasse quelque chose contre l'ordre."

This general, and, if I may call it so, *possible* sort of *probability*, may be termed, *the probability of romance;* and these lines of Agatho furnish a good apologetical motto for the novel writer. It might be prefixed, perhaps, without impropriety, even to the best productions of the kind—to a CLARISSA, or a CECILIA. Nothing is so commonly complained of in such works, as their *improbability;* and often, no doubt, the complaint is well-founded : often, however, the criticism means nothing more, than that the events are *uncommon*, and proves nothing more, than the want of fancy, and an extended view of human life, in the reader. If the events were *not* uncommon, where would the book find readers ? Twining.

posed by bad poets indeed, through their own want of ability[5]; but by good poets, on account of the players[6]. For, introducing [dramatic] contests, and extending the plot beyond its capabilities, they are frequently compelled to distort the connexion of the parts. But, since tragedy is not only an imitation of a perfect action, but also of actions which are terrible and piteous, and actions principally become such, [and in a greater degree, when they happen contrary to opinion,[7]] on account of each other. * * * * For thus they will possess more of the marvellous, than if they happened from chance and fortune; since, also, of things which are from fortune, those appear to be most admirable, which seem to happen as it were by design. Thus the statue of Mityus at Argos, killed him who was the cause of the death of Mityus by falling as he was surveying it.[8] For such events as these seem not to take place casually. Hence it is necessary that fables of this kind should be more beautiful.

11. Definition of the terrible.

12. Of chance circumstances.

CHAP. X.

Fables either simple or compound.

1. Of fables simple and complex.

OF fables, however, some are simple, and others complex; for so also are the actions of which fables are the imitations. But I call the action *simple*,

---

[5] Such is the sense of δι' αὐτοὺς="*propter ingenii tarditatem.*" Ritter.

[6] i. e. that the play may not show off only one actor. Thus a modern dramatist writes a play for Charles Kean, and puts in a few episodes for Buckstone or Keeley. It is clear from this that plays were often written to suit particular performers.

[7] These words are condemned as interpolated. But the apodosis to the whole sentence is wanting, and I have therefore marked the lacuna with Ritter.

[8] A similar story of the death of a cruel beloved being killed by the falling of a statue of Cupid, is told by Theocritus, Id xxiii. sub fin.

from which taking place, as it has been defined,
with continuity and unity, there is a transition without either revolution or *discovery;* but complex, from
which there is a transition, together with discovery,
or revolution, or both.   It is necessary, however, 3.
that these should be effected from the composition
itself of the fable, so that from what has formerly
happened it may come to pass that the same things
take place either necessarily or probably.   For it
makes a great difference whether these things are
effected on account of these, or after these.

CHAP. XI.

Now, revolution is a mutation, as has been stated, of 1. Defini-
actions into a contrary condition ; and this, as we say, tion of re-
according to the probable, or the necessary.   Thus volution ;
in the " Œdipus,[1] " the messenger who comes with an
intention of delighting Œdipus and liberating him
from his fear respecting his mother, when he makes
himself known, produces a contrary effect.   Thus,
too, in the "Lynceus," he indeed is introduced as one
who is to die, and Danaus follows with an intention
of killing him ; but it happens from the course of incidents, that Lynceus is saved, and Danaus is slain.
And discovery is, as the name signifies, a change 2. of dis-
from ignorance to knowledge, or into the friendship covery.
or hatred of those who are destined to prosperous or
adverse fortune.   The discovery, however, is most
beautiful, when at the same time there are, as in the
"Œdipus,[2]" revolutions.   There are, therefore, other 3. Other
discoveries also.   For sometimes it happens, as has recogni-
been before observed, that there are discoveries of tions.
things inanimate[3], and casual ; or if some one has

---

[1] Cf. Soph. Œd. Tyr. 1014, sqq. Dind.
[2] Such is the *discovery* of Joseph by his brethren, Gen. xlv.
—the most beautiful and affecting example that can be given.
Twining.
[3] I do not understand Aristotle to be here speaking of *such*

performed, or has not performed, a thing, there is a
recognition of it; but the discovery which especially
pertains to the fable and the action is that before

4. Feelings excited by revolution and discovery.

mentioned. For a discovery and revolution of this
kind will excite either pity or fear; and tragedy is
supposed to be an imitation of such actions [as excite
fear and pity]. Again, it will happen that infelicity and felicity will be in such like discover-

5. Different discoveries.

ies. But since discovery is a discovery of certain
persons, some [discoveries] are of one person only
with reference to another, when it is evident who the
other person is, but sometimes it is necessary to discover both persons. Thus Iphigenia was recognised
by Orestes through the sending an epistle[4]; but
another discovery was requisite to his being known

6. The third requisite is pathos or disaster.

by Iphigenia[5]. [Two parts of the fable, therefore, viz.
revolution and discovery, are conversant with these
things; but the third part is pathos. And of these,
revolution and discovery have been already discussed.
Pathos, however, is an action destructive, or lamentable; such as death when it is obvious, grievous pains,
wounds, and such like particulars[6].]

CHAP. XII.

On the Parts of Tragedy.

1. The parts of tragedy according to quantity.

[BUT we have before spoken of the parts of tragedy
which are requisite to constitute its quality. The
parts of tragedy, however, according to quantity, and

discoveries of "inanimate things" (rings, bracelets, etc.) as are
the means of bringing about the true discovery—that of the
persons. For, in what follows, it is implied that these "other
sorts of discovery" produce neither terror nor pity, neither hap-
piness nor unhappiness; which can by no means be said of such
discoveries as are instrumental to the personal discovery, and,
through that, to the catastrophe of the piece. Of these, he
treats afterwards.—Dacier, I think, has mistaken this. Twining.

4 Cf. Eur. Iph. Taur. 759. 92.   5 Ibid. 811. 26.

6 The whole of this paragraph is condemned by Ritter.

into which it is separately divided, are as follow :
prologue,[1] episode,[2] exode,[3] and chorus, of the parts
of which one is the *parodos*,[4] but the other is the *stasimon*.[5] These [five] parts, therefore, are common
to all [tragedies]; but the peculiar parts are [the
songs] from the scene and the *kommoi*. And the
prologue, indeed, is the whole part of the tragedy,
prior to the entrance of the chorus. The episode is
the whole part of the tragedy between two complete
odes of the chorus. The exode is the whole part of
the tragedy, after which there is no further melody
of the chorus. And of the chorus, the parodos, indeed, is the first speech of the whole chorus; but the
stasimon is the melody of the chorus, without ana-
pæst and trochee: and the commos[6] is the common
lamentation of the chorus and from the scene. But
we have before shown what the parts of tragedy are
which must necessarily be used; but the parts of it
according to quantity, and into which it is separately
divided, are these[7].]

(marginal notes:) 2. Pro-logue. Episode. Exode. Parodos. Stasimon. Commos. 3.

¹ *Prologue*—This may be compared to our *first act.* See
note 40. Twining.

² *Episode*—i. e. *a part introduced, inserted,* etc., as all the
dialogue was, originally, between the choral odes. Twining.

³ *Exode*—i. e. the *going out,* or *exit;* the concluding *act,* as
we should term it. The Greek tragedies never *finished* with a
choral ode. Twining.

⁴ *Parode*—i. e. *entry* of the chorus upon the stage : and
hence the term was applied to *what they first sung,* upon their
entry. Twining.

⁵ *Stasimon*—i. e. *stable ;* because, as it is explained, these
odes were sung by the choral troop when fixed on the stage,
and at rest : whereas the *parode* is said to have been sung *as
they came on.* Hence, the *trochaic* and *anapæstic* measures,
being lively and full of motion, were adapted to the *parode,* but
not to the *stasimon.* Twining.

⁶ From a verb signifying to *beat* or *strike ;* alluding to the
gestures of violent grief.

⁷ Ritter, who has illustrated this whole chapter with great
learning and taste, allows its utility, but doubts that it is the
work of Aristotle. The reader will find his remarks on the
different parts of tragedy very valuable.

CHAP. XIII.

The Essentials for a Tragic Plot.

1. In the next place we must show, as consequent to what has been said, what those who compose fables ought to aim at, and beware of, and whence the purpose of tragedy is effected. Since, therefore, it is necessary that the composition of the most beautiful tragedy should not be simple, but complex, and that it should be imitative of fearful and piteous actions—(for this is the peculiarity of such imitation)—in the first place it is evident, that it is not proper that worthy men should be represented as changed from prosperity to adversity, (for this is neither a subject of terror nor commiseration, but is impious,) nor should depraved characters [be represented as changed] from adversity to prosperity; for this is the most foreign from tragedy of all things, since it possesses nothing which is proper; for it neither appeals to moral sense[1], nor is piteous, nor fearful. Nor, again, must a very depraved man be represented as having fallen from prosperity into adversity. For such a composition will indeed possess moral tendency, but not pity or fear. For the one is conversant with a character which does not deserve to be unfortunate; but the other, with a character similar [to one's own]. [And pity, indeed, is excited for one who does not deserve to be unfortunate; but fear, for one who resembles oneself[2]]; so that the event will neither appear to be commiserable, nor terrible. There remains therefore the character between these. But a character of this kind is one, who neither excels in virtue and justice, nor is changed through vice and depravity, into misfortune, from a state of

2. Tragedy should not be simple. Proper vicissitudes.

3. The character of the hero must be of a moderate

---

[1] Ritter considers τὸ φιλάνθρωπον as a feeling bordering on ἔλεος, "id quidem quod prope ad miserationem accedit." It probably is best expressed by our "humanity," considered in both its senses.

[2] Ritter condemns these words as a marginal annotation.

great renown and prosperity, but has experienced this change through some [human] error; such as Œdipus and Thyestes, and other illustrious men of this kind. Hence it is necessary that a plot which is well constructed, should be rather single[3] than twofold, (though some say it should be the latter,) and that the change should not be into prosperity from adversity, but on the contrary into adversity from prosperity, not through depravity, but through some great error, either of such a character [as we have mentioned], or better rather than worse. But the proof of this is what has taken place. For of old the poets adopted any casual fables; but now the most beautiful tragedies are composed about a few families; as for instance, about Alcmæon, Œdipus, Orestes, Meleager, Thyestes, and Telephus[4], and such other persons as happen either to have suffered or done things of a dreadful nature. The tragedy, therefore, which is most beautiful according to art, is of this construction. Hence they erroneously blame Euripides, who accuse him of having done this in his tragedies, and for making many of them terminate in misfortune. For this method, as we have said, is right; of which this is the greatest evidence, that in the scenes, and contests of the players, simple fables which terminate unhappily appear to be most tragical, if they are properly acted. And Euripides, though he does not manage other things well, yet appears to be the most tragic of poets[5]. The fable, however, ranks in the second place, though by some it is said to be the first composition, which has a twofold construction, such as the Odyssey, and which terminates in a contrary fortune, both to the better

excellence or depravity.

4. Simple fable preferable to twofold.

5. Proof from the popular subjects of tragedy.

6. An unhappy end most suitable to tragedy,

7. but least popular,

[3] What is here meant by a *single* fable, will appear presently from the account of its opposite—the *double* fable. It must not be confounded with the *simple* fable, though in the original both are expressed by the same word. The *simple* fable is only a fable *without revolution, or discovery*. Twining.

[4] The same remark applies to the French tragic stage.

[5] But below, xv. 5. and Eth. iii. 1, Euripides is justly charged with the improper introduction of comic characters and language. The praise applies only to the catastrophe.

and worse characters. It appears, however, to rank in the first place, through the imbecility of the spec-

8. and the happy conclusion preferred.

tators[6]. For the poets, in composing their plots, accommodate themselves to the wish of the spectators. This pleasure, however, is not [properly] derived from tragedy, but is rather suited to comedy. For there, though the greatest enemies be introduced, as Orestes and Ægisthus, yet in the end they depart friends, and no one falls by the hand of the other[7].

CHAP. XIV.

Of Terror and Pity.

1. Terror and pity, how produced.

TERROR and pity, therefore, may be produced from the sight[1]. But they may also arise from the com-

[6] That weakness which cannot bear strong emotions, even from fictitious distress. I have known those who could not look at that admirable picture, the *Ugolino* of Sir Jos. Reynolds.—To some minds, every thing that is not *cheerful* is *shocking.*—But, might not the preference here attributed to *weakness*, be attributed to better causes—the gratification of philanthropy, the love of justice, order, etc. ?—the same causes which, just before, induced Aristotle himself to condemn, as *shocking* and *disgusting*, those fables which involve the virtuous in calamity. Twining.

Modern audiences partake of this weakness. Thus, the catastrophe of "Measure for Measure," "Cymbeline," or "Winter's Tale," are more satisfactory than those of "Hamlet" or "Pizarro." Knowles's "Hunchback" is a happy specimen of ἀναγνώρισις, leading to a happy termination, while his "Wife" displeases. Marston's "Heart and the World," weak as the play is, is more agreeable than his "Patrician's Daughter." But such plays are merely serious comedies.

[7] This is excellently applicable to the plays of Vanbrugh and Cibber. Compare the conclusions of the "Relapse," (Sir Tunbelly excepted,) the "Provoked Wife," etc. As to the ἀποθνήσκει οὐδεὶς ὑπ' οὐδενος, it is very descriptive of the *duels* in a modern or ancient comedy, as in "London Assurance," or in the "Beaux Stratagem," according to Scrub's description.

[1] See a very pleasant paper of Addison's on this subject, "Spectator," No. 42. We know the effect of the skull and

bination of the incidents, which is preferable, and the province of a better poet. For it is necessary that the fable should be so composed, that he who hears the things which are transacted, may be seized with horror, and feel pity, from the events, without the assistance of the sight; and in this manner any one who hears the fable of Œdipus is affected. But to effect this through spectacle is more inartificial, and requires great expense[2]. But they who produce not the terrible, but the monstrous alone, through scenic representation, have nothing in common with tragedy. For it is not proper to expect every kind of pleasure from tragedy, but that which is appropriate. Since, however, it is necessary that the poet should procure pleasure from pity and fear through imitation, it is evident that this must be effected by the circumstances. Let us, then, ascertain what kind of events appear to be dreadful or lamentable. But it is necessary that actions of this kind should either be those of friends towards each other, or of enemies, or of neither. If, therefore, an enemy kills an enemy, he does not show any thing which is an object of pity, neither while he does the deed, nor when he is about to do it, except what arises from the deed itself. And this will be the case, when one of those who are neither friends nor enemies do the same. But when these things happen in friendships[3], as when a brother kills a brother, or a son his father, or a mother her son, or a son his mother, or intends to do it, or does any thing else of the like kind—such subjects are to be sought for. One must not, therefore, [completely] alter the received fables. I mean, for instance, such as the fable of Clytemnestra being slain by Orestes, and of

2. The monstrous not tragic.

3. The proper pleasure to be derived from tragedy.

4. What actions are dreadful or lamentable.

5. Further pre-

---

black hangings in the " Fair Penitent," the scaffold in " Venice Preserved," the tomb in " Romeo and Juliet," etc. Twining. But Ritter understands ὄψις to mean the countenance of the actor.

[2] " Χορηγίαν generatim pro *pretioso et operoso apparatu* et apte dici posse et eo intellectu h. l. accipiendam esse manifestum est." Ritter.

[3] As in the " Fatal Curiosity " of Lillo. Twining.

cepts re-
specting
fable.

6. Exam-
ples.

Eriphyle by Alcmæon. But it is necessary that the
poet should invent the plot, and use in a becoming
manner those fables which are handed down. What,
however, we mean by [using fables] in a becoming
manner, let us explain more clearly. Now, the action
may take place in such a way as the ancients have
represented it, viz. knowingly with intent ; as Euripides represents Medea killing her children. Men
may also do an action, who are ignorant of, and
afterwards discover their connexion [with, the in-
jured party,] as in the "Œdipus" of Sophocles.
This, therefore, is extraneous to the drama[4], but is
in the tragedy itself ; as in the "Alcmæon" of As-
tydamas, or Telegonus in the "Ulysses Wounded[5]."

7. Further still, besides these there is a third mode,
when some one is about to perpetrate, through ignorance, an atrocious deed, but makes the discovery
before he does it[6]. And besides these there is no
other mode. For it is necessary to act, or not ; and
that knowing, or not knowing. But of these, to in-
tend to perpetrate the deed knowingly, and not to
perpetrate it, is the worst ; for it is wicked and not
tragical ; because it is void of pathos. [Hence, no
poet introduces a character of this kind except
rarely ; as in the "Antigone," in which Hæmon
[endeavours to kill his father] Creon, [but does not

---

[4] The murder of Laius by Œdipus, his son, is supposed to
have happened a considerable time before the beginning of the
action. Twining.

[5] Of these two dramas nothing more is known than the little
that Aristotle here tells us. In the first, the poet adhered so
far to history, as to make Alcmæon *kill* his mother Eriphyle,
but with the improvement, (according to Aristotle's idea,) of
making him do it *ignorantly*. The story of *Telegonus* is, that
he was a son of Ulysses by *Circe;* was sent by her in quest of
his father, whom he wounded, without knowing him, in a
skirmish relative to some sheep, that he attempted to carry off
from the island of Ithaca. It is somewhat singular, that the
wound is said to have been given with a kind of *Otaheite* spear,
headed with a sharp fish-bone. See Pope's Odyssey, xi. 167,
and the note. Twining.

[6] Thus in Talfourd's "Ion," Ion discovers Adrastus to be
his father, just as he is on the point of murdering him.

effect his purpose.][7]] For the action here ranks in
the second place. But it is better to perpetrate the 8.
deed ignorantly, and having perpetrated to discover;
for then it is not attended with wickedness, and the
discovery excites horror. The last mode, however, 9.
is the best; I mean, as in the "Cresphontes," in
which Merope is about to kill her son, but does not,
in consequence of discovering that he was her son.
Thus, too, in the "Iphigenia in Tauris," in which
the sister is going to kill the brother, [but recognises him;] and in the "Helle," the son is about to
betray his mother, but is prevented by recognising
her. Hence, as has been formerly observed, trage- 10.
dies are not conversant with many families; for
poets were enabled to discover incident of this kind
in fables, not from art, but from fortune[8]. They 11.
were compelled, therefore, to direct their attention
to those families in which calamities of this kind
happened.

And thus we have spoken sufficiently concerning
the combination of the incidents, and have shown
what kind of fables ought to be employed.

CHAP. XV.

W TH respect to manners, however, there are four 1. Requi-
things to which one ought to direct attention: one, sites of
indeed, and the first, that they be good. But the manners,
tragedy will indeed possess manners, if, as was said, that they
the words or the action render any deliberate inten- express
tion apparent; containing good manners[1], if the προαίρε-
deliberate intention is good. But manners are to be σις,
found in each genus; for both a woman and a slave
may be good; though perhaps of these, the one is

---

[7] Ritter condemns this passage. See also Donaldson, Introduction to the Antigone, p. xl.

[8] i. e. to history or tradition.

[1] The interpolation φαῦλον μὲν ἐὰν φαύλη ᾖ is rightly thrown
out by Ritter.

2. that they be adapted to the persons,

3. similar,

4. and consistent.

5. Depraved manners unnecessary.

less good[2], and the other is wholly bad[3]. In the second place, the manners must be adapted to the persons. For there are manners which are characterized by fortitude, but it is not suited to a woman to be either brave or terrible. In the third place, the manners must be similar. For this, as was before observed, differs from making the manners to be good and adapted[4]. In the fourth place, they must be uniform ; for if he is anomalous, who exhibits the imitation, and expresses such like manners, at the same time it is necessary that he should be uniformly unequal. The example, however, of depraved manners is indeed not necessary ; such, for instance, as that of Menelaus in the " Orestes," but an example of unbecoming and unappropriate manners is, the lamentation of Ulysses in the tragedy of " Scylla,[5]" and the speech of Menalippe ; and the example of anomalous manners in the Iphigenia in Aulis. For Iphigenia

[2] This is very Euripidean gallantry. Compare Aristoph. 546, sqq.

[3] This is observed, to show the consistence of this *first* precept with the next. The manners must be drawn *as* good as may be, consistently with the observance of *propriety*, with respect to the *general* character of different sexes, ages, conditions, etc. It might have been objected—" You say the character must be *good*. But suppose the poet has to represent, for instance, a slave ?—the character of slaves in general is notoriously *bad*."—The answer is,—*any thing* may be good *in its kind*. Twining.

[4] This is very trivial, compared with Horace's description of the manners suited to different characters. Cf. Ars Poet. 114, sqq.

[5] Of the Scylla nothing is known.—Some fragments remain of "Menalippe the Wise," (for this was the title,) a tragedy of Euripides, the subject of which is a curiosity. *Menalippe* was delivered of two children, the fruits of a stolen amour with *Neptune*. To conceal her shame, she hid them in her father's *cow-house ;* where he found them, and being less of a philosopher than his daughter, took them for a monstrous production of some of his cows, and ordered them to be burned. His daughter, in order to save them, without exposing herself, enters into a long physical argument, upon the principles of *Anaxagoras*, to cure her father of his unphilosophical prejudices about monsters and portentous births, and to convince him that these infants *might* be the *natural* children of his cows. Twining.

supplicating does not at all resemble the Iphigenia in the latter part of the tragedy. It is requisite, however, in the manners as well as in the combination of the incidents, always to investigate, either the necessary or the probable; so that such a person should say or do such things, either necessarily or probably; and that it be necessary or probable, that this thing should be done after that. It is evident, therefore, that the solutions of fables ought to happen from the fable itself, and not as in the " Medea,[6]" from the machinery, and in the tragedy called the "Iliad," from the particulars respecting the sailing away [from Troy[7]]. But we must employ machinery in things which are external to the drama, which either happened before, and which it is not possible for men to know, or which happened afterwards, and require to be previously foretold and announced. For we ascribe to the gods the power of seeing all things, but we do not admit the introduction of any thing absurd in the incidents[8], but if it is introduced it must be external to the tragedy; as in the "Œdipus" of Sophocles. Since, however, tragedy is an imitation of better things, it is necessary that we should imitate good painters. For these, in giving an appropriate form to the image, depict the similitude, but increase the beauty[9]. Thus, also, it is requisite that the poet, in imitating the wrathful and the indolent, and those who are similarly affected in their manners, should form an example of equity, or asperity; such as Agatho and Homer have represented Achilles. These things, indeed, it is necessary to observe; and besides these, such perceptions of the senses as are attendant upon poetry, besides

Margin notes:
6. Necessity and probability of action.
7. Solution ought to be from the fable, not the machinery.
8. Comparison with painting.
9.

---

[6] Of Euripides. *Medea* is carried off, at the end of the tragedy, in a chariot drawn by flying dragons. Twining.

[7] Pope's Iliad, ii. 189, etc. Twining.

[8] By *incidents of the fable*, Aristotle here plainly means all those actions or events which are *essential parts* of the *subject* or *story*, whether previous to the action, and necessary to be known, or included in it, and actually represented *in* the drama.

[9] This seems intended to explain his *third* precept, of *resemblance* in the manners; to reconcile it with his *first*, and to show what *sort* of likeness the nature of tragic imitation requires. Twining.

the necessary ones.[10] For in these, errors are frequently committed. But concerning these things, enough has been said in the treatises already published.

CHAP. XVI.

1. On the different recognitions.

[[1]WHAT discovery, however, is, has been before stated. But with respect to the species of recognition, the first indeed is the most inartificial, and that which most poets use through being at a loss, and is effected

2. through signs. But of these, some are natural, such as the "lance with which the earth-born[2] race are marked," or the stars [on the bodies of the sons] in the "Thyestes" of Carcinus. Others are adventitious, and of these some are in the body, as scars; but others are external, such as necklaces; and such as [the discovery] through a small boat, in the

3. Their use.

"Tyro[3]." These signs also may be used in a better or worse manner. Thus Ulysses,[4] through his scar, is in one way known by his nurse, and in another by the swineherds. For the discoveries which are for the sake of credibility, are more inartificial, and all

[10] i. e. to the *sight*, and the *hearing*; in other words, to actual *representation*.

[1] The reader, who recollects the conclusion of Sect. 14, where the author took a formal leave of the "*fable* and *its requisites*," and proceeded to the *second* essential part of tragedy, the *manners*, will hardly be of Dacier's opinion, who contends that this section is rightly placed. His reasons are perfectly unsatisfactory. Twining. I have enclosed it in brackets, with Ritter.

[2] The descendants of the original Thebans, who, according to the fabulous history, sprung from the earth when Cadmus sowed the dragon's teeth, etc.—This *noble race* are said to have been distinguished by the natural mark of a lance upon their bodies.

[3] Sophocles wrote two tragedies of this name, neither of them preserved.—The story of Tyro leads us to suppose, that Aristotle means the little boat, trough, or, as some render it, *cradle*, in which Tyro had exposed her children, on, or near, the river: the particular manner of the discovery it would be in vain to guess.

[4] See Pope's Odyssey, xix. v. 451, etc., and the note there, on v. 461, and xxi. 226.

of them are of this kind; but those which are from revolution, as in the "Washing of Ulysses[5]," are better. And those recognitions rank in the second place, which are invented by the poet, on which account they are inartificial. Thus Orestes in the "Iphigenia" discovers that he is Orestes[6]. For she indeed recognises her brother through a letter, but Orestes himself speaks what the poet designs, but not what the fable requires; on which account it is near to the above-mentioned error; since he might have introduced some [of the real things as signs]. Thus, too, in the "Tereus" of Sophocles, the "voice of the shuttle" [produced a recognition[7]]. But the third mode of discovery is through memory, from the sensible perception of something by sight, as in the "Cyprii" of Dicæogenes; for on seeing the picture a certain person weeps. And in the "Tale of Alcinous;" for Ulysses, on hearing the lyrist, and recollecting the story, weeps; whence also [all these] were recognised. The fourth mode of discovery is derived from syllogism[8], as in the "Choephoræ"—a person like

4. Invented recognitions.

5. By memory.

6. By reasoning.

---

[5] The ancients distinguished the different parts of Homer's poems by different titles accommodated to the different subjects, or episodes; and, in referring to him, they made use of these, not of the division into *books*. Thus, the part of the xixth book of the Odyssey above referred to, was called *The Washing*. The *Tale of Alcinous* was another title, which will presently be mentioned. Twining.

[6] I follow Ritter, who supplies "to Iphigenia." The older editors interpolated the passage. See Ritter's note on the following passage. The whole disputation is "arguta et obscura," as the learned critic observes.

[7] Taylor's note is pre-eminently absurd. Tyrwhitt elegantly explains the passage thus: κερκίδος φωνή is a quotation from the play, and denotes the *web itself*, by means of which Philomela explained to her sister Procne the injuries she had suffered from Tereus, since, her tongue being cut out, she could not speak. Cf. Ovid, Met. VI. 424; Hygin. Fab. 45, quoted by Ritter, whose note deserves the student's attention. As the web is said to *speak*, which *describes*, so the shield of Capaneus χρυσοῖς φωνεῖ γράμμασιν, Æsch. Sept. C. Th. 434.

[8] *Occasioned* by reasoning;—i. e. by reasoning, (or rather, *inference*, or *conclusion*,) *in the person discovered.* See the note.—It should be remembered, that Aristotle is not, in this chapter, *inventing* discoveries, nor enumerating all the kinds

me is arrived—there is no person like me but
Orestes,—Orestes, therefore, is arrived. Thus too
in the "Iphigenia[9]" of Polyides the sophist. For it
was probable that Orestes would syllogistically con-
clude, that because his sister had been immolated,
it would likewise happen to him to be sacrificed.
Thus also in the "Tydeus[10]" of Theodectes, a certain person comes to discover his son, and himself
perishes[11]. Another example also is in the "Phinidæ."
For the women, on seeing the place, inferred what
their fate would be, viz. that they must needs perish
in this place; for they were exposed in it from their
infancy. There is also a certain compound [dis-
covery], which is produced from the false inference
of the spectator, as in the "Ulysses the False Messenger." For he says, he should know the bow, which
he had not seen; but the [audience], as if he must
be known through this, on this account infer falsely.
The best recognition, however, of all, is that which
arises from the things themselves, astonishment being
excited through probable circumstances; as in the
"Œdipus" of Sophocles and the "Iphigenia;" (for
it is probable that she would be willing to send letters;)
since such things alone are without fictitious signs and
necklaces[12]. But the recognitions which rank in the
second place, are those which are derived from syllogism.]

7. By the misconception of the audience.

8. The best is from the circumstances themselves.

possible or practicable; but only classing and examining such
as he found in use, or could recollect, in the tragedies and epic
poems of his time. Twining.

[9] The subject appears to have been the same as that of the
Iphigenia in Tauris of Euripides. We are to suppose, that
Orestes was discovered to his sister by this natural exclama-
tion, at the moment when he was led to the altar of Diana to
be sacrificed. Twining.

[10] Of this and the preceding tragedy, we know nothing but
what we learn here: i. e. that in the one, *a father*, and in the
other, the *daughters* of *Phineus*, were discovered, and, probably, saved, by those exclamations. Twining.

[11] See Ritter. Nothing of this play is known.

[12] All this passage is hopelessly corrupt.

CHAP. XVII.

It is necessary, however, that the poet should form 1. Rules
the plots, and elaborate his diction, in such a manner for re-
that he may as much as possible place the thing before $\frac{\text{alizing}}{\text{ideas.}}$
his own eyes[1]. For thus] the poet perceiving most
acutely, as if present with the transactions themselves,
will discover what is becoming, and whatever is re-
pugnant will be least concealed from his view. An
evidence of this is the fault with which Carcinus is
reproached. For Amphiaraus had left the temple,
which was concealed from the spectator, who did not
perceive it, and the piece was driven[2] from the stage
in consequence of the indignation of the spectators.
For the poet as much as possible should co-operate
with the gestures [of the actor] ; since those are
naturally most adapted to persuade who are themselves under the influence of passion. Hence, also, 2. The
he agitates others who is himself agitated[3], and he poet
excites others to anger who is himself most truly $\frac{\text{should}}{\text{feel what}}$
enraged. Hence, poetry is the province either of he writes,
one who is naturally clever, or of one who is insane[4].

---

[1] i. e. place himself in the position of a spectator. Ritter
observes that σόν συνίστανται must be supplied.

[2] ἐκπίπτειν is properly used of the condemnation of a piece.
See Hemst. on Lucian, Nigrin. § 8. In Demosth. de Coron.
p. 315, ed. Reisk. it is applied to the actor. Cf. Bud. Com.
L. Gr. p. 536. There is a pun upon the double meaning of
the verb. Amphiaraus went (ἐξέπεσε) away, and the piece
was condemned (ἐξέπεσε) in consequence.

[3] But Twining, in a long and learned note, expresses his
opinion that χειμαίνει may be used in its proper neuter sense,
and that the meaning may be as follows : " The poet should
work himself, as far as may be, into the passion he is to represent, by even assuming the countenance and the gestures
which are its natural expressions. For they, of course. have
most probability and truth in their imitation, who actually feel,
in some degree, the passion : and no one *expresses agitation* of
mind (χειμαίνει) so naturally, (ἀληθινώτατα,) as he who is
really agitated, (χειμαζόμενος,) or *expresses* anger (χαλεπαίνει)
so naturally, as he who is really angry (ὀργιζόμενος)."

[4] " In an enthusiasm allied to madness," is Twining's
translation, which is all that Aristotle means to say, under-

For of these characters, the one is easily fashioned,
but the other is prone to ecstasy. It is likewise
necessary that the poet should in a general way lay
down the fables composed by others, and those which
he composes himself, and afterwards introduce episodes and lengthen out [the play]. But I say that
he should give a general sketch after this manner.
Thus, for instance, in the "Iphigenia[5]," a certain
virgin on the point of being sacrificed, and vanishing
from the view of those who were to sacrifice her, and
being brought to another country in which it was a
law to sacrifice strangers to a certain goddess, she
is appointed the priestess of these rites. Some time
after, it happened that the brother of the priestess
came to this place; [but on what account? Because
some god had ordered him, for a certain reason which
does not pertain to the general view of the tragedy,]
to come thither, [but why he did so is foreign to the
fable[6]]. The brother, therefore, coming, and being
made captive, discovered [his sister], when he is
going to be sacrificed; whether, as Euripides says, [by
an epistle,] or, as Polyides feigns, speaking according
to probability, because he said, it was not only requisite that the sister, but that he also should be sacrificed:—and hence safety arises. After these things,
the poet having given names to the persons, should
insert the episodes; and he must be careful that the
episodes be appropriate; as that of the insanity
through which Orestes was taken captive, and his
being saved through expiation. In dramas, therefore,
the episodes are short, but by these the epopee is
lengthened. For the fable of the Odyssey is short, viz.
a certain man wandering for many years, and perse-
cuted by Neptune, and left alone. And besides this,
his domestic affairs being so circumstanced, that his

3. and
should
form a
general
sketch of
his plot.

4. The
episodes
must be
suitable

5. and
short.

standing " eos, qui animo commotiores sunt," as Ritter renders it. On the connexion between poetic enthusiasm and
madness, cf. Plato, Ion. p. 145. C. etc. Phædr. p. 344. B. Læm.
with Clemens Alex. Strom. vi. p. 927. Theodoret. θεραπ. II. p.
25. Cicer. de Div. I. 37.
    [5] Eur. Iph. Taur.
    [6] The passage is interpolated. See Ritter.

wealth is consumed by suitors, and stratagems are plotted against his son. But driven by a tempest, he returns, and making himself known to certain persons, he attacks the suitors, and is himself saved, but destroys his enemies. This, therefore, is the peculiarity of the fable, but the rest is episode.

CHAP. XVIII.

[In every tragedy, however, there is a complication and development[1]. And external circumstances indeed, and some of those that are internal, frequently form the complication; but the rest the development. I call, however, the complication, the whole of that which extends from the beginning to the last part, from which there is a transition to good fortune; but I call the development that part which extends from the beginning of the transition to the end. Thus in the Lynceus of Theodectes, the past transactions, and the capture of the son, are the complication; but the part which extends from the charge of murder to the end, is the development. But of tragedy there are four species; for so many parts of it have also been enumerated. And one species is the complicated, of which the whole is revolution and discovery; another, the pathetic, such as the tragedies of Ajax and Ixion; another, the moral[2], such as the Phthiotides and the Peleus; but the

1. Complication and development.

2. Four species of tragedy;

---

[1] Literally, the *tying* and *untying*. With the French, *Nœud* and *Denouement* are convenient and established terms. I hope I shall be pardoned for avoiding our awkward expressions of the *intrigue* and *unravelling* of a plot, etc. I could find no terms less exceptionable than those I have used. Twining.

[2] i. e. in which the delineation of *manners* or *character* is predominant. Our language, I think, wants a word to express *this* sense of the Greek ἠθικὸν, and the Latin, *moratum*. *Mannered* has, I believe, sometimes been used in this sense; but so seldom, as to sound awkwardly. We know nothing of the subjects here given as examples. Twining.

fourth is another such as the "Phorcides[3]" and the "Prometheus," and the tragedies which represent

3. all which the poet should understand.

what passes in Hades. It is especially necessary, therefore, that the poet should endeavour to have all these species; or at least that he should have the greatest and most of them, especially since men of the present age calumniate the poets. For as there have been good poets in each part of tragedy, they now expect one poet to excel in all the parts. But it is right to call tragedy different and the same, though not perhaps with any reference to the fable; but this [may be the case with those] of which there is the same plot and solution. But many poets complicate well, and develope badly[4]. But both these should always be applauded[5]. But it is necessary to recollect, as has been often observed, that we must

4. On epic tragedy.

not make tragedy an epic system. Now, I call that tragedy an epic system, which consists of many fables; as if some one should compose a tragedy from the whole fable of the Iliad. For in the Iliad, on account of its length, the parts receive an appropriate magnitude. But in dramas, the effect produced would be very contrary to expectation. The

5. Illustrations.

truth of this is indicated by such as have represented [in one tragedy] the whole destruction of Troy, and not some part of it, as the "Niobe" or "Medea" of Euripides, and who have not acted like Æschylus; for these have either been condemned,

[3] *Æschylus* wrote a tragedy so named. It is difficult to imagine what he could make of these three curious personages, who were *born old women*, lived under ground, and had but one eye among them, which they used by turns; carrying it, I suppose, in a case, like a pair of spectacles. Such is the tale! Twining.

[4] No fault so common : see note 59. It was with the Greek tragedians, probably, as with *Shakspeare*.—"In many of his plays the latter part is evidently neglected. When he found himself near the end of his work, and in view of his reward, he shortened the labour, to snatch the profit. He therefore remits his efforts where he should most vigorously exert them, and his catastrophe is improbably produced, or imperfectly represented." Johnson's Pref. to Shakspeare. Twining.

[5] This passage is contradictory and unintelligible. See Ritter, who condemns the whole as spurious.

or contend without success ; since Agatho also failed
in this alone.   But in revolutions, and in simple actions, those poets admirably effect their aim.   For
this is tragical, and has a moral tendency.   This, 6.
however, takes place when a wise but a depraved
man, such as Sisyphus, is deceived; and a brave but
unjust man is vanquished.   But this is probable, as
Agatho says.   For it is probable that many things
may take place contrary to probability.   It is neces- 7. The
sary likewise to conceive the chorus to be one of the business
players[6] and a part of the whole, and that it co-oper- of the
ates with the players, not as in Euripides[7], but as in chorus.
Sophocles.   But with other tragedians, the choral
songs do not more belong to that fable, than to any
other tragedy; on which account the chorus sing
detached pieces, inserted at pleasure[8], of which Agatho was the inventor.   What difference, however,

---

[6]   *Actoris* partes chorus, *officiumque virile*
        Defendat : neu quid *medios intercinat actus*,
        Quod non proposito conducat et *hæreat aptè*.
                                        Hor. A. P. 193.

[7] This expression does not, I think, necessarily imply any
stronger censure of *Euripides*, than that the choral odes of his
tragedies were, in general, more loosely connected with the
subject, than those of *Sophocles ;* which, on examination,
would, I believe, be found true.   For that *this* is the fault here
meant, not the improper " *choice of the persons who compose
the chorus*," as the ingenious translator of Euripides understands, is, I think, plain from what immediately follows; the
connexion being this :—" *Sophocles* is, in this respect, *most*
perfect; Euripides *less* so ; as to the *others, their* choral songs
are *totally foreign* to the subject of their tragedies."   See Pot-
ter's Euripides—Postscript to the Trojan Dames.   Warton's
Essay on the Genius, etc., of Pope, vol. i. p. 71.

[8] It is curious to trace the gradual extinction of the chorus.
At first, it was *all ;* then, relieved by the intermixture of dialogue, but still *principal ;* then, *subordinate* to the dialogue;
then, digressive, and *ill connected* with the piece ; then, borrow-
ed from *other pieces* at pleasure—and so on, to the fiddles and
the act-tunes, at which Dacier is so angry.   (See his note, p.
335.)   The performers in the *orchestra* of a modern theatre
are little, I believe, aware, that they occupy the *place*, and may
consider themselves as the lineal descendants, of the ancient
chorus. Orchestra (ὀρχηστρα) was the name of that part of the
ancient theatre which was appropriated to the chorus.   [Jul.
Pollux, IV. p. 423.]

does it make, to sing inserted pieces, or to adapt the diction of one drama to another, or the whole episode?

CHAP. XIX.

1. Diction and sentiment. OF the other parts of tragedy enough has now been said. But it remains that we should speak concerning the diction and the sentiments. The particulars, therefore, respecting the sentiments, are unfolded in the treatise on Rhetoric, to which it more properly belongs. But those things pertain to the sentiments, which it is requisite to procure by a reasoning process. And the parts of these are, to demonstrate, to

2. Their parts. refute, and to excite the passions; such as pity, or fear, or anger, and such like; and besides these, to

3. amplify and extenuate. It is evident, however, that in things, also, it is requisite to derive what is useful from the same forms, when it is necessary to procure objects of pity, or things that are dreadful, or great, or probable. Except that there is this difference, that things in tragedy ought to be rendered apparent without teaching, but in an oration they are to be shown by the speaker, and in consequence of the speech. For what employment would there be for the orator, if the things should appear [of themselves]

4. How far the poet should be pleasing, and not through the speech? But of things pertaining to diction, there is one species of theory respecting the forms of speech [1], which it is the pro-

---

[1] What are we to understand by these σχήματα λέξεως?—The learned reader will immediately see, that, as Victorius has observed, they are not to be confounded with those σχήματα λέξεως, of which we hear so much from Cicero, Quintilian, Dion. Hal. etc.,—those "figuræ *verborum*," which are opposed to the σχήματα διανοίας, the "figuræ *mentis, sententiarum*," etc. Indeed, no such division of σχήματα is, I believe, to be found in Aristotle. It seems to have been the invention of the later rhetoricians; and how little they were agreed, as to the number and the species of these σχήματα, the propriety of the division itself, and even the precise sense of the *word* σχῆμα, may be seen in Quintilian ix. 1.—The σχήματα λέξεως of Aris-

vince of the actor to know, and of him who is a master artist in this profession. Thus, for instance, [it is requisite he should know,] what a mandate is, what a prayer, narration, threats, interrogation and answer are, and whatever else there may be of this kind. For from the knowledge or ignorance of these, the poetic art incurs no blame of any moment. For who would think that Homer errs in what he is reproved for by Protagoras? viz. that while he fancies he prays, he commands, when he says, " The wrath, O goddess, sing." For, says he, to order a thing to be done, or not to be done, is a mandate. Hence, this must be omitted as a theorem pertaining to another art, and not to poetry.

(margin: acquainted with the different applications of diction. 5.)

CHAP. XX.

The parts of Diction.

[¹ OF all diction, however, the following are the parts; viz. the letter, the syllable, the conjunction, the noun, the verb, the article, the case, and the sentence. The

(margin: 1. The parts of diction.)

totle in this place, are plainly such as would have been denominated by later writers, σχήματα διανοίας—figures of the *thought* or *sense*. Indeed we find them actually enumerated among the figures of that class. See Dionys. Halicarn. de Struct. etc. Sect. 8.—So Quintilian ; " *Figuras* quoque *mentis*, quæ σχήματα διανοίας dicuntur, res eadem recipit omnes, in quas nonnulli diviserunt species dictorum, (i. e. of *jokes, bons mots*). Nam et *interrogamus*, et dubitamus, et affirmamus, et *minamur*, et *optamus*."

I see, therefore, not the least reason why the expression σχῆμα λέξεως should not be rendered here exactly as in the other passages above referred to, " *figura orationis* "—*form*, or *configuration, of speech*. For λέξις, it must be observed, is here used, not in the particular sense of *diction*, or *style* and *manner of expression*, (as it is used Rhet. iii. 8,) but in the general sense of λόγος, *speech*, as we find it used in the beginning of the next chapter.

¹ This chapter is an evident interpolation, and the student will gain but little benefit from its perusal, as the matter of it is incorrect and ill arranged. See Ritter.

2. Letters.   letter, therefore, indeed, is an indivisible sound[2]; yet
not every such sound, but that from which an intelli-
gible sound is adapted to be produced. For there
are indivisible vocal sounds of brutes, no one of which
3. Their   I call a letter[3]. But the parts of this indivisible
divisions,   sound are, vowel, semivowel, and mute. And a
vowel, indeed, is that which has an audible sound,
without percussion[4]; such as *a* and *o*. But a semivowel is that which has an audible sound, with percussion; as *s* and *r*. And a mute is that which,
even with the concurrence of the tongue, has of itself,
indeed, no sound, but becomes audible in conjunction
with things which have a certain sound; as *g* and
4. and dif-   *d*. But these differ by the configurations of the
ferences.   mouth, in the parts [of the mouth[5]] by density and
tenuity of aspiration, by length and shortness; and
further still, they differ by acuteness and gravity,
and by the medium between both these; the theory
respecting each of which pertains to the metrical
5. Sylla-   art. But a syllable is a sound without signification,
bles.   composed from a mute, and an element which has
sound [i. e. from a vowel, or semivowel]. For *g r*
without *a* is a syllable[6], and also with *a*, as *g r a*.

[2] "Vocal sound," is Taylor's translation of φωνή.

[3] "Element of diction." Taylor.

[4] As Hermann has ventured to call προσβολὴ *allisus*, I
trust I shall be excused for adopting Twining's quaint, but
clear translation. He observes: "Literally, *percussion*, i. e.
of the tongue against the palate, or teeth, the lips against the
teeth, or against each other, and all the other modes of *conso-
nant* articulation. See Hermes, iii. 2. p. 322, where they are
called '*contacts*.' Dacier makes sad confusion here, both in
his version and his notes, by confounding the *names* of the
consonants, when vowels are prefixed, or put after them, to
make them *separately pronouncible*, (Te, eF, eL, etc.,) with
their powers *in composition*—as elements of *words*. Thus, it
is strictly true, that S and R have *a sound*, without the assistance of a vowel, merely by their mode of articulation. But D,
or G, have no sound at all *by themselves*. The semivowels
are l, m, n, r, s. (Dion. Halicarn. De Struct. Orat. sect. 14.) "

[5] i. e. the different organs of speech, from which letters are
denominated nasal, dental, labial, etc. Taylor.

[6] *G r* is an instance of a syllable composed of a mute and a
semivowel; and *g r a* of a syllable composed of a mute, a
vowel, and a semivowel. Taylor. But see Ritter.

The study, however, of the differences of these, pertains also to the metrical art. But a conjunction is 6. Con-
a sound void of signification, which neither impedes junction.
nor produces one significant sound adapted to be
composed from many sounds, and which may be
placed either at the beginning or the end of the period, unless something requires that it should be
placed by itself at the beginning; such as μὲν, ἤτοι,
δή. Or it is a sound without signification, composed
from more sounds than one, but naturally adapted to
produce one significant sound. An article is a sound 7. Article
without signification, which shows the beginning, or
end, or distinction of a word[7]; as τὸ φημί, and τὸ
περί, and others of the like kind. Or it is a sound
without signification, which neither impedes nor produces one significant sound naturally adapted to be
composed from many sounds, both in the extremes and
in the middle. But a noun is a composite sound, 8. Noun.
significant without time, of which no part is of itself
significant. For in double nouns, we do not use the
parts as of themselves significant. Thus, in the word
Theodorus, [though *Theos* signifies God and *doron* a
gift,] yet *doron* signifies nothing. A verb is a com- 9. Verb.
posite sound, significant with time, of which no part
is of itself significant, in the same manner also as in
nouns. For *man* or *white* does not signify time; but
he walks, or *he did walk,* signify, the former indeed
the present, and the latter the past time. But case 10. Case.
pertains to noun or verb. And one case, indeed,
[in nouns] signifies that something is said *of* this
thing, or is attributed *to*[8] this thing, and the like;

[7] This description is most obscure; but the sense seems to
be, that an article is a sound which of itself does not signify
any thing definite, but merely serves to indicate a significant
sound, before or after which it is placed, or which it distin-
guishes from other words. Taylor. Ritter denies that there
is any sense at all, an opinion in which the reader will probably acquiesce.

[8] These *only,* in *modern* grammar, are called *cases*: in Aristotle, *number,* whether in noun or verb, and the *tenses,* and
modes, (or *moods,*) of verbs, are comprehended under that
term; because *cases* (πτωσεις—*cases*) are *endings, terminations, inflections,* etc., and, in the learned languages, *all* the

but another is that which pertains to one thing or many things; as *men*, or *man*. And another case pertains to acting[9], such as what relates to interrogation or demand. For *did he walk?* Or *walk* is a case of a verb according to these species. And a

11. Sentence. sentence is a composite significant sound, of which certain parts of themselves signify something; for not every sentence is composed from nouns and verbs, (since the definition of man[10] is a sentence without a verb,) but there may be a sentence without verbs. A sentence, however, will always have some part significant; as in the sentence *Cleon walks*, the word Cleon is significant. But a sentence is one in

12. Its unity. a twofold respect; for it is either that which signifies one thing, or that which becomes one from many by conjunction[11]. Thus the Iliad, indeed, is one by conjunction; but the definition of man is one, because it signifies one thing.]

CHAP. XXI.

On Nouns and Metaphors.

1. The species of nouns. WITH respect to the species of a noun, one is simple; and I call the simple noun that which is not com-

above-mentioned differences of meaning are expressed by different *terminations*. The French use *chute*, the literal translation of *casus*, in the sense of *termination*—"La chute d'une periode," etc. And *fall* is used, in our poetical language, for a close, or *cadence*, in music.

That strain again—it had a dying FALL.

Merch. of Venice.

And so Milton in Comus, v. 251. Twining.

[9] These *modes* are the same which he calls *figures* of *speech*, Sect. 23. Twining.

[10] The definition alluded to appears to be this, literally rendered: "*A terrestrial animal with two feet*" (ζῷον πεζὸν, δίπουν). Twining.

[11] Compare περὶ Ἑρμην. cap. v. p. 38.—Analyt. Post. lib. ii. cap. 10. p. 469, E.—Metaphys. vii. 4. p. 910, D. (where he uses τῷ συνέχει, as equivalent to συνδέσμῳ,) and viii. 6. p.

posed from significant parts; but another is twofold. And this either consists of that which is significant, and that which is without signification, or
of both parts significant. A noun also may be triple
and quadruple, as is the case with many of the nouns
of the Megaliotæ[1]; such as *Hermocaïcoxanthus*[2].
But every noun is either proper or foreign[3], or me- 2. Their
taphorical, [or ornamental[4],] or invented, or ex- divisions
tended, or contracted, or altered. But I call that a 3. Pro-
proper name, which is used by every one; and that per and
a foreign[5] name which is used by other nations. foreign.
Hence it is evident that the same noun may be both
foreign and proper, though not to the same people.
For the word Σίγυνον[6] is proper to the Cyprians,

931, C. Twining. Ritter remarks, that the compiler of this
chapter did not understand the passages he copied.
  [1] I have read, in some ludicrous book, of a country that was
"*lost by the ignorance of geographers.*" This seems to have
been the case of these *Megaliotæ*, if such a people ever ex-
isted. They are no where recorded.—Dacier reads, μεγαρι-
ζόντων—" ceux qui *disent de grandes choses :*" and cites *Hesy-
chius*—Μεγαρίζοντες—μεγαλα λέγοντες. But this is too distant
from the present reading, Μεγαλιωτῶν. Winstanley's conjecture—μεγαλείων, ὡς, is somewhat nearer, and, in other respects, preferable : but it is, I think, a strong presumption
against its truth, that Aristotle constantly uses οἷον, when he
gives an instance ; never, as far as I recollect, ὡς.
  I have sometimes thought it not very improbable, that the
passage might originally have stood thus : τῶν μέγαλΑ Διω-
ΚΟΝτων : i. e. of those who *affect, aim at,* are *fond of,*
grandeur and pomp of expression ; who *love hard words,* as
we say. Nothing more common than this sense of διωκειν.
Twining.
  Donaldson, Theatre of the Greeks, p. 27, pt. 2, adopts Tyrwhitt's conjecture, μεγαλείων ὡς, as being confirmed by
Xenoph. Mem. II. 1, § 34, and renders it, "the bombastic
expressions." Ritter prefers πολλαπλομεγάλωπος, as an *example* of this kind of word, but Donaldson seems right.
  [2] This is a noun composed from the names of the three
rivers Hermus, Caicus, and Xanthus.
  [3] Cf. Rhet. iii. 1 and 2.
  [4] Ritter condemns the addition of κόσμος, as it has no definition.
  [5] Ritter remarks that γλῶτται are both *provincialisms* and
obsolete words.
  [6] i. e. *a spear.*

4. Metaphor.

5. Different metaphors exemplified.

6. Analogous.

but foreign to us. But a metaphor[7] is the transposition of a noun from its proper signification, either from the genus to the species, or from the species to the genus; or from species to species, or according to the analagous. I call, however, a transposition from genus to species, such as,

> Secure in yonder port my vessel stands[8].

For to be moored is a species of standing. But a transposition from species to genus is such as,

> ————Ten thousand valiant deeds
> Ulysses has achieved[9].

For ten thousand is a great number, and is now used instead of many. And a transposition from species to species is such as,

> The brazen falchion drew away his life.

And,

> Cut by the ruthless sword[10].

For here *to draw away*, is used instead of *to cut;* and *to cut* is used instead of *to draw away;* since both imply the taking something away. But I call it analogous, when the relation of the second term to the first is similar to that of the fourth to the third; for then the fourth is used instead of the second, or the second instead of the fourth. [And sometimes the proper term is added to the relative terms[11].] I say, for instance, a cup has a similar relation to Bacchus that a shield has to Mars. Hence, a shield may be called the cup of Mars, and a cup the shield of Bacchus. Again, evening has the same relation to day that old age has to life. One may therefore say that

---

[7] Aristotle understands *metaphor* in a more extended sense than we do, for we only consider the third and fourth of the kinds enumerated by him, as metaphors. Our usurpation of the word was in vogue in Cicero's time. See de Orat. III. 38, sqq. Ritter.

[8] Odyss. A. 185.   [9] Il. B. 272.

[10] This, and the next species only, answer to what we call *metaphor*—the metaphor founded on *resemblance*. The two first species belong to the trope denominated, since Aristotle's time, *Synecdoche*. Twining.

[11] This is perfectly out of place and useless. See Ritter.

evening is the old age of day, and that old age is the
evening of life ; or as Empedocles calls it, "The set-
ting of life [12]." In some instances, also, where there
is no analogous name, this method may be no less
similarly employed. Thus, to scatter grain is to sow ;
but there is no name for the scattering of light from
the sun, and yet this has a similar relation to the sun
that sowing has to grain. Hence, it is said,

7. Means
of em-
ploying
them.

————Sowing his god-created flame.

This mode of metaphor may likewise be used differently, when, calling a thing by a foreign name, something belonging to it is denied of it ; as if one should
call a shield not the cup of Mars, but the wineless
cup. But an invented noun is that, in short, which,
not being adopted by others, is introduced by the poet
himself. For it appears that there are certain nouns
of this kind ; as substituting ἔρνυγες instead of κέρατα
for *horns* [13], and calling a *priest* ἀρητήρ [14], instead of
ἱερεύς. And a word is extended or contracted, partly
by using a vowel longer than the proper one, or by
inserting a syllable ; and partly by taking something
away from it. An extended noun, indeed, is such as
πόληος for πόλεως, and πηληϊάδεω for πηλείδου ; but
the contracted, such as κρῖ, and δῶ [15] ; and,

8.

9. Inven-
ted words.

10. Ex-
tended
and con
tracted.

————μία γίνεται ἀμφοτέρων ὄψ [16].
————The sight of both is one.

And a word is changed when the poet leaves part of
it, and invents part ; as,

11.
Changed.

[12] "Thy *sun* is *set*, thy spring is gone."
                                    Gray, Ode on Spring.
"Yet hath my *night of life* some memory."
        Shakspeare, Com. of Errors—last scene. Twining.
[13] i. e. *branches ;* which we also use for the *horns* of a stag.
But Aristotle means a *new word*, not a *new application* merely
of a word already in use. Twining.
[14] A *supplicator ;* literally, a *prayer*, taken in the sense of *one
who prays ;* as *seer* is used for *prophet*. Twining.
[15] Κρῖ is used Il. E. 196. Δῶ, Il. A. 425. Twining.
[16] Part of a verse of Empedocles, quoted by Strabo, p. 364,
ed. Cantab.

Δεξιτερὸν κατὰ μαζόν.
In the right breast [17].

12. On genders. Instead of δεξιόν. [[18]Further still, of nouns some are masculine, others feminine, and others between, [or neuter]. And the masculine, indeed, are such as end in ν, and ρ, and σ, and such as are composed from σ; but these are two, ψ and ξ. The feminine nouns are such as are composed from vowels, and always end in long vowels; as, for instance, in η and ω, or in α of the doubtful. Hence it happens that the number of terminations for masculine and feminine are equal; for the terminations of ψ and ξ are the same. No noun, however, ends in a mute, or in a short vowel; and only three nouns end in ι, viz. μέλι, κόμμι, and πέπερι. But five end in υ; viz. πῶϋ, νᾶπυ, γόνυ, δόρυ, and ἄστυ. And the neuter nouns end in these, and in ν and ς.]

CHAP. XXII.

The subject of Diction continued.

1. Two requisites of diction, clearness, and freedom from meanness, How produced. THE virtue of diction, however, consists in being perspicuous, and not mean[1]. The diction, therefore, is most perspicuous, which is composed from proper nouns, but then it will be mean. But an example of this is the poetry of Cleophon and Sthenelus. It will, however, be elevated, and remote from the vulgar idiom, by employing unusual words. But I call unusual words, such words as are foreign, the metaphorical, the extended, and every word except the proper [name of a thing]. If, however, [a poet] **2. Results and effects of the different kinds of words.** wholly employ such words as these, it will be either an enigma, or a barbarism. If, therefore, it were

[17] Il. E. 393.
[18] This following passage is false in its statements, and totally foreign to Aristotle's design. Ritter, therefore, has rightly condemned it.
[1] Cf. Rhet. iii. 1, extr. and 2. init.

composed from metaphors, it would be an enigma; but if from foreign words, a barbarism. For the essence of an enigma is this, to unite things impossible, yet really true². Now, from the arrangement of the words, it is not possible to effect this, but it may be effected by a metaphor; as "I saw a man who had glued brass to a man with fire³;" and others of the like kind. [But from the composition of foreign words a barbarism is produced⁴.] Hence language should be moderately varied with these. Foreign, 3. therefore, metaphorical, [and ornamental] words, and the other species that have been mentioned, will cause the diction to be neither vulgar nor mean; but proper words produce perspicuity. But the extend- 4. ing, contracting, and changing of names, contribute in no small degree to the perspicuity of the diction, without vulgarity. For the use of words in a way different from their proper and usual signification, causes the diction to be not vulgar; but the adoption of words in their accustomed meaning, renders it perspicuous. Hence those do not blame rightly, who 5. Objec- find fault with this mode of speech, and like the an- tions ill founded. cient Euclid ridicule the poet, [objecting] that verse might easily be composed, if one permit the quantity of syllables to be lengthened at pleasure, making Iambics even in common discourse; as

ἤτοι Χάριν εἶδον Μαραθῶννάδε βαδίζοντα.

And,

Οὐκ ἄν γ᾿ ἐράμενος τὸν ἐκείνου ἐλλέβορου⁵.

---

² τὸ λέγοντα ὑπάρχοντα ἀδύνατα συνάψαι, "to put together things apparently inconsistent and impossible, and at the same time saying nothing but what is true." Twining.
³ Rhet. iii. 2. κόλλησιν εἶπε τὴν τῆς σικύας προσβολήν. The operation of cupping is meant. Compare Celsus ii. 11, and Almelov. on Cœlius Aurel. Chronic. ii. 1. § 394. Rhod. on Scribon. Larg. Compos. xlvi. The fire alludes to the burnt tow (linamentum) used to exhaust the air in the cupping glass.
⁴ Apparently a gloss. See Ritter.
⁵ It is of little use to attempt to settle the reading of these "nonsense verses." Ritter observes that the fault probably lay in pronouncing βαδδίζοντα, ἐρράμενος. See his notes.

6. It is evident, therefore, that to be detected using this
mode of diction is ridiculous. [But measure is common to all the parts of diction [6].] For it would produce the same effect, to make an improper and
ridiculous use of metaphors, foreign words, and other
7. forms of diction. But how great a difference is
made by the appropriate use of them, may be seen in
epic poetry, by putting the words in metre. And he
who transfers proper names into foreign words, into
metaphors, and the other forms, will see that what we
have said is true. Thus, for instance, Æschylus
and Euripides made the same Iambic verse; but by
only changing one word from its proper and usual
to a foreign signification, the one verse appears
beautiful, and the other mean. For Æschylus indeed, in his Philoctetes, writes,

A cancerous ulcer feeds upon my foot.

But Euripides, instead of ἐσθίει, *feeds*, uses the word
θοινᾶται, *banquets on.* And,

Νῦν δέ μ' ἐὼν ὀλίγος τε καὶ οὐτιδανὸς καὶ ἄκικυς,

by inserting proper [and common] words, it will be,

Νῦν δέ μ' ἐὼν μικρός τε καὶ ἀσθενικὸς καὶ ἀειδής[7].

And,

Δίφρον ἀεικέλιον καταθεὶς, ὀλίγην τε τράπεζαν.
Δίφρον μοχθηρὸν καταθεὶς, μικράν τε τράπεζαν [8].

[6] Twining renders, "in the employment of all the species
of unusual words, moderation is necessary." But this meaning
can scarcely be elicited from the words. See Ritter, who condemns the passage as an interpolation.
[7] In this verse Polyphemus complains that he was deprived
of sight by Ulysses, a *little, weak, vile* man. But Homer, instead of using the word μικρὸς, *little*, uses ὀλίγος, which signifies *few*. Instead of ἀσθενικὸς, *puny*, he uses οὐτιδανὸς, which
signifies a man of no account; and ἄκικυς, *powerless*, instead
of ἀειδὴς, *obscure*. Taylor. Cf. Od. ix. 515.
[8] In this verse, which is from the 21st book of the Odyssey,
Homer, for the purpose of signifying an *ignoble seat*, calls it by
a foreign word, ἀεικέλιον, and not by the usual word, μοχθηρόν;
and he calls the *table*, not μικράν, *small*, but ὀλίγην, *few*.
Taylor. Cf. Od. xxi. 259.

Or change, ἠϊόνες βοόωσιν (the shores rebellow[9]) to ἠϊόνες κράζουσιν (the shores cry out). [[10] Again, Ariphrades used to ridicule the tragic poets for employing modes of diction, which no one would use in common conversation; such as δωμάτων ἄπο, and not ἀπὸ δωμάτων, i. e. *home from*, and not *from home;* σέθεν [for σοῦ]; ἐγὼ δέ νιν[11], and Ἀχιλλέως πέρι, and not περὶ Ἀχιλλέως, i. e. *Achilles about*, and not *about Achilles;* and other expressions of the like kind. For all such forms of language, because they are not in common use, remove vulgarity from the diction. But this he did not know.] It is, however, a great thing to use each of the above-mentioned modes in a becoming manner; and also compound and foreign words. But the greatest thing is to employ metaphors well. For this alone cannot be acquired from another, but it is an indication of an excellent genius; since to employ metaphors well, is to discern similitude[12]. But of words, the compound are chiefly suited to dithyrambic verse, the foreign to heroic, and metaphors to Iambic verse. And in heroic verse, indeed, all the above-mentioned words are useful; but in Iambics, because they especially imitate common discourse, those words are adapted which may be also used in conversation. And words of this description are, the proper, the metaphorical, [and the ornamental.] And thus much may suffice concerning tragedy, and the imitation in acting[13].

8. Further objections answered.

9. Proper use of the different words,

10. as suited to each kind of poetry.

---

[9] Il. P. 265.—Pope's line is,
    "And distant rocks *rebellow* to the roar." Twining.
[10] Ritter objects to this clause. Twining, however, admires and commends its conclusion.
[11] Cf. Soph. Œd. col. 987.
[12] More clearly expressed in Rhet. iii. 11. 5, τὸ ὅμοιον καὶ ἐν πολὺ διέχουσι θεωρεῖν, εὐστόχου.
[13] These last words appear to me out of place.

CHAP. XXIII.

On the Epic Poem.

1. On narrative poetry. Its similarity to tragedy. CONCERNING the poetry, however, which is narrative and imitative in metre, it is evident that it ought to have dramatic fables, in the same manner as tragedy, and should be conversant with one whole and perfect action, which has a beginning, middle, and end, in order that, like one whole animal, it may produce its appropriate pleasure[1]; and that it may not be like the custom of histories, in which it is not necessary to treat of one action, but of one time, viz. of such things as have happened in that time, respecting one or more persons, the relation of each of which things 2. to the other is just as it may happen. For as the sea-fight at Salamis, and the battle with the Carthaginians in Sicily, though they happened at the same time, tend nothing to the same end; thus also in successive times, one thing may sometimes be connected with another, from which no one end is produced.

3. Praise of Homer, and comparison with other poets. But nearly all poets do this. Hence, as we have before observed, in this respect also Homer will appear to be divine, when compared with other poets, because he did not attempt to sing of the whole of the Trojan war, though it had a beginning and an end. For if he had, it would have been very great, and not sufficiently conspicuous; or if it had been of a moderate size, it would have been intricate through the variety of incidents[2]. But now, having selected one part of the war, he has made use of many episodes; such as the catalogue of the ships, and other episodes, with which he has adorned his

---

[1] i. e. opposed (as appears from what follows) to that which *history* gives. *Unity* of *interest* is essential to the pleasure we expect from the epic poem; and this cannot exist, at least in the degree required, without *unity* of *action*. Twining.

[2] Because "*the length of the whole would*" then "*not admit of a proper magnitude in the parts;*" and thus an *epic poem* constructed upon an *historical plan*, would be exactly in the same case with a *tragedy* "constructed on an *epic plan*." Twining.

poem.   Other poets, however, have composed a fable about one man, and one time, and one action, consisting of many parts; as the authors of the Cypriacs, and the Lesser Iliad [3].   [With respect to the Iliad [4]. and Odyssey, therefore, one or two tragedies only could be made from each.   But many might be made from the Cypriacs; and from the Lesser Iliad more than eight; such as the Judgment of the Arms [4], Philoctetes [5], Neoptolemus, Eurypylus [6], the Begging [of Ulysses], the Lacænæ, the Destruction of Troy, the Return of the Greeks, Sinon, and the Troades.

CHAP. XXIV.

On the Species, Parts, etc. of Epic Poetry.

AGAIN, it is requisite that the epopee should have the same species as tragedy.   [For it is necessary that it should be either simple, or complex, or ethical, or pathetic [1].]   The parts also are the same, except the music and the scenery.   For it requires revolutions, discoveries, and disasters ; and besides these, the sen-

1. The species and parts of epic poetry.

[3] Of this kind seems the poem of *Ariosto*, the *exordium* of which not only expresses the miscellaneous variety of his matter, but, also, his *principle* of *unity*.

> Le Donne, i cavalier, l' arme, gli amori,
> Le cortesie, l' audaci imprese, io canto,
> *Che furo al* TEMPO che passaro i Mori, etc.

Ariosto's expedient was, to "intertwist the several actions together, in order to give something like the appearance of one action" to the whole, as has been observed of *Spenser* [*Letters on Chivalry*, etc.]: he has given his poem the continuity of basket-work.   Or, if I may be indulged in another comparison, his unity is the unity produced between oil and vinegar by shaking them together, which only makes them *separate by smaller portions*.   Twining.

[4] So called to distinguish it from the *Iliad* of Homer, of which it seems to have been a continuation.   Twining.

[5] i. e. between Ajax and Ulysses.   *Æschylus* wrote a tragedy on this subject, of which the *Ajax* of Sophocles is the sequel.   Dacier.

[6] Of these two plays nothing is known.

[1] Condemned by Ritter.

timents and the diction should be well formed; all
which were first used by Homer, and are used by him

2. Differ- fitly.   For of his two poems, the Iliad indeed con-
ence be- tains the simple and pathetic; but the Odyssey, the
tween the complex; for through the whole of it there is dis-
Iliad and
Odyssey. covery[2] and moral.   And besides these things, he
3. Length excelled all poets in diction and sentiment.   The
of the   epopee, however, differs from tragedy in the length
epic
poem.   of the composition, and in the metre.   But the proper boundary of its length has been before described;
for it should be such that the beginning and the end
may be seen at one view.   [And this will be effected
if the compositions are shorter than those of the ancient poets, and brought to the same length with the
multitude of tragedies that are recited at one hear-

4. Its   ing[3].]   But it is the peculiarity of the epopee to
power of   possess abundantly the power of extending its mag-
extension. nitude; for tragedy is not capable of imitating many
actions that are performed at the same time, but that
part only which is represented in the scene, and
acted by the players.   But in the epopee, in consequence of its being a narration, many events may be
introduced which have happened at the same time,
which are properly connected with the subject, and
from which the bulk of the poem is increased.   Hence,
this contributes to its magnificence, transports the
hearer to different places, and adorns the poem with
dissimilar episodes.   For similitude of events rapidly

5. Its   produces satiety, and causes tragedies to fail.   But
proper   heroic metre is established by experience as adapted
metre.   to the epopee.   For if any one should attempt narrative imitation in any other metre, or in many

---

[2] See Pope's translation, xvi. 206, etc., where Ulysses discovers himself to Telemachus—xxi. 212, to the shepherds—
xxiii. 211, to Penelope—xxiv. 375, to his father—ix. 17,
to Alcinous—iv. 150, etc., Telemachus is discovered to Menelaus by his tears—v. 189, to Helen, by his resemblance to
his father—xix. 545, Ulysses is discovered to the old nurse,
by the scar.   Twining.

[3] This is quite contrary to Aristotle's own opinion. See Ritter.   Twining's great and tasteful learning cannot bring him
to any satisfactory explanation of these words.

metres mingled together, the unfitness of it would be
apparent. For heroic metre is of all others the most
stable and ample. [Hence it especially receives
foreign words and metaphors. For narrative imitation excels all others[4].] But Iambics and tetrametres
have more motion; the one being adapted to dancing,
but the other to acting. It would, however, be still
more absurd, to mingle them together, as Chæremon[5]
did. Hence, no one has composed a long poem in
any other measure than the heroic; but, as we have
said, Nature herself teaches us to distinguish the
measure best suited. Homer, indeed, deserves to be
praised for many other things, and also because he is
the only poet who was not ignorant what he ought
to do himself. For it is requisite that the poet
should speak in his own person as little as possible;
for so far as he does so he is not an imitator.[6] Other
poets, therefore, take an active part through the
whole poem, and they only imitate a few things, and
seldom[7]. But Homer, after a short preface, immediately introduces a man or a woman, or something
else[8] that has manners; for there is nothing in his
poem unattended with manners. It is necessary,
therefore, in tragedies to produce the wonderful; but
that which is contrary to reason (whence the wonderful is best produced) is best suited to the epopee,
from the agent not being seen[9]. In the next place,
the particulars respecting the pursuit of Hector

6. Ob-
scurity of
mixed
metres.

7. Praise
of Homer.

8. The
wonder-
ful con-
sidered in
reference
to tragedy
and
epopee.

---

[4] Condemned by Ritter.   [5] Cf. i. 9.

[6] *Strictly* speaking. See Dissertation i. p. 37. Twining.

[7] This is remarkably the case with *Lucan;* of whom Hobbes
says, that "no heroic poem raises such admiration of *the poet*
as his hath done, though not so great admiration of the *persons*
he introduceth." — [Discourse concerning the Virtues of an
Heroic Poem.] Twining.

[8] As gods, goddesses, allegorical beings, etc. Twining.

[9] The best comment to which I can refer the reader upon
all this part of Aristotle, is to be found in the 10th of the *Letters on Chivalry and Romance,* in which the *Italian* poets, and
the privileges of genuine poetry, are vindicated, with as much
solidity as elegance, against those whom Dryden used to call
his "*Prose Critics,*"—against that sort of criticism "*which
looks like philosophy, and is not.*"—Dr. Hurd's Dialogues, etc.
vol. iii. Twining.

would appear ridiculous in the scene; the Greeks indeed standing still, and not pursuing, and Achilles making signs to them, by the motion of his head, not to engage[10]. But in the epopee this is concealed. Now, the wonderful pleases; of which this is an indication, that all men, when they wish to gratify their hearers, add something to what they relate. Homer also in the highest degree taught others how to feign in a proper manner. But this is a paralogism. For men fancy that when the consequent follows or results from the antecedent, the consequent may be converted, and that the antecedent will follow from the consequent. This, however, is false. [But why, if the antecedent be false, so long as this other be otherwise, should the consequent necessarily follow? For through knowing the consequent to be true, our soul paralogizes, and concludes that the antecedent also is true. And there is an example of this in "the Washing[11]."] Again, one should prefer things which are impossible but probable, to such as are possible but improbable. Fables also should not be composed from irrational parts, [but as much as possible, indeed, they should have nothing irrational in them: if, however, this is impossible, care should be taken that the irrational circumstance does not pertain to the fable, as in the case of Œdipus not knowing how Laius died[12]. For it must not be brought into the drama, like the narration of the Pythian games in the Electra[13], or him who, in the tragedy of the

9. False reasonings respecting poetry.

10. Further precepts respecting poetic probability.

[10] Pope's Iliad, xxii. 267.—Perhaps the idea of stopping a whole army by a nod, or shake of the head, (a circumstance distinctly mentioned by Homer, but sunk in Mr. Pope's version,) was the absurdity here *principally* meant. If this whole Homeric scene were represented on our stage, in the best manner possible, there can be no doubt that the effect would justify Aristotle's observation. It would certainly set the audience in a roar. Twining.

[11] I follow Ritter's text and version, but both he and Donaldson regard these words as an interpolation.

[12] Cf. Soph. Œd. Tyr. 112, sqq. This clause is condemned by Ritter.

[13] Id. Electr. 680, sqq. See my Introduction to Sophocles, p. xiii.

Mysians, comes from Tegea to Mysia without speaking.] It is ridiculous, therefore, to say, that otherwise the fable would be destroyed; for such fables
should not at first be composed. But if they are
composed, and it appears more reasonable that they
should be, the absurdity also must be admitted;
since the irrational circumstances in the Odyssey,
such as Ulysses being left [on the shore of Ithaca by
the Phœacians], would evidently have been intoler-
able, if they had been fabricated by a bad poet. But
now the poet conceals the absurdity, and renders it
pleasing by the addition of other beauties. The diction, likewise, should be laboured in the sluggish
parts of the poem, and which exhibit neither manners
nor sentiment[14]. For a very splendid[15] diction conceals the manners and the reasoning.

11. The diction in the respective parts.

CHAP. XXV.

On removing critical Objections.

[WITH respect to critical objections[1], and the solutions of them, the number and quality of their species

1. Objections of critics,

[14] The reader may wonder that Aristotle did not add—"nor
passion." But that part of the epic and tragic poem, which
he calls the *sentiments*, includes the *expression of passion.*
Twining.

[15] "His diction [*Thomson's*] is in the highest degree florid
and luxuriant; such as may be said to be to his images and
thoughts *both their lustre and their shade;* such as invests them
with splendour, through which perhaps they are not always
easily discerned."—*Dr. Johnson's Life of Thomson.* Twining.

[1] The original is, *Problems.* This appears to have been a
common title of critical works in Aristotle's time. Objections,
censures, and the most unreasonable cavils, were conveyed in
the civil form of *problems* and *questions.* Thus, many criticisms on *Homer* were published under the title of *Homeric
Problems.*

The scope of this part of Aristotle's work is of more importance to his subject than, at first view, it may appear to be.
In teaching how to *answer* criticisms, it, in fact, teaches, (as
far, I mean, as it goes,) what the poet should do to avoid

and their will become apparent from surveying them as follows.
solutions. Since the poet is an imitator, in the same manner as
a painter, or any other person who makes likenesses,
it is necessary that he should always imitate one of
the three [objects of imitation]. For he must either
imitate things such as they were or are, or such as
they are said and appear to be[2], or such as they
2. ought to be. But these are enunciated either by
[common] diction, or by foreign words and metaphors. For there are many modifications[3] of diction;
3. Error and we concede these to the poets. Besides this,
twofold, there is not the same rectitude of politics and poetry,
essential
and acci- nor of any other art and poetry. But of poetry itself,
dental. the error is twofold; the one essential, the other
4. accidental. For the error is essential, when it attempts to imitate that which is beyond its power;
but [when it attempts to imitate improperly, as[4]] if,
for instance, a horse should be described as moving
both its right legs together, or an error in any of the

giving occasion to them. It seems, indeed, intended as an
apology for *Poetry*, and a vindication of its privileges upon true
poetical principles, at a time when the art and its professors
were unfairly attacked on all sides, by the cavils of *prosaic*
philosophers and sophists, such as *Ariphrades, Protagoras,
Euclid*, etc., and by the *puritanical* objections of PLATO and his
followers. Twining.

If Ritter's strictures be true, our acquaintance with *Aristotle's*
Poetics is now at an end. In a learned annotation (pp. 263—6)
he seems to have completely proved the spurious character of
both this and the following chapter.

[2] This includes all that is called *faery, machinery*, ghosts,
witches, enchantments, etc.— things, according to *Hobbes*,
"beyond the actual bounds, and only within the "*conceived
possibility* of nature." [See the *Letters on Chivalry*, as above.]
Such a being as *Caliban*, for example, is *impossible*. Yet
Shakspeare has made the character *appear probable;* not, certainly, to *reason*, but to *imagination;* that is, *we make no difficulty about the possibility* of it, in *reading*. Is not the *Lovelace*
of Richardson, in this view, more out of nature, more improbable, than the *Caliban* of Shakspeare? The latter is, at least,
consistent. I can *imagine* such a monster as Caliban: I never
could imagine such a man as Lovelace. Twining.

[3] πάθη, inflections, dialectic variations, etc.

[4] These words, τὸ προελέσθαι μὴ ὀρθῶς, are totally inconsistent with the meaning. See Ritter.

arts be committed in poetry, as in medicine, or any
other art, when it fabricates things that are impossible, these, therefore, whatever they may be, are not
the *essential* errors of poetry. Hence, one must re- 5.
fute the objections of critics from surveying these Whence
particulars. For in the first place, indeed, the poet may be
errs, if what he fabricates is impossible according to removed.
the art itself ; but it will be right if the end of poetry is obtained by it. For we have before shown
what the end is, viz. if the poet thus renders what
he fabricates, or any other part of the poem, more
capable of producing a more striking effect[5]. An
example of this is the pursuit of Hector. If, however, this end can be more or less attained, and that
according to the art pertaining to these things, then
the fault will not be excusable. For it is requisite
if possible to be entirely without error. Further
still, it should be considered whether the error ranks
among things essential to the poetic art, or foreign
and incidental. For it is a less fault not to know
that a hind has no horns, than to depict a bad copy
of one. Besides this, also, if the poet is blamed for 6.
not imitating things as they truly are, the reply is,
but he imitates them as they should be. Thus Sophocles said, that he described men such as they
should be, but Euripides such as they are. If, however, it should be objected, that the poet represents
things in neither of these ways, he may say that he
represents them as men say they are ; as, for instance, in things pertaining to the gods. For per- 7.
haps it is neither better thus to speak, nor true, but
it is just as it may happen ; as Xenophanes observes,
" At any rate they tell us such things[6]." Perhaps,
however, it may be said, that it is not better, indeed,
thus to speak, but that the thing was so ; as in the
passage concerning the arms [of the sleeping soldiers of Diomed] :

---

[5] A false definition. See Ritter.

[6] " Tyrwhitt's emendation, ἀλλ' οὖν φασὶν τάδε, seems to be
the best of those which have been proposed." Donaldson.

ἔγχεα δέ σφιν ὄρθ' ἐπὶ σαυρωτῆρος,

————fixed upright in the earth
Their spears stood by————[7]

For such was the custom at that time, as it is now
8. with the Illyrians. With respect, however, to the
inquiry whether a thing is said or done by any one
well or ill, we must not only regard the thing itself
which is done or said, whether it is good or bad, but
we must also [consider] the person by whom it is done
or said, viz. concerning whom, or when, or to whom, or
on what account, he speaks or acts ; as whether it is
for the sake of bringing to pass a greater good, or in
9. Dic- order to avoid a greater evil. But it is requisite to
tion.   remove some objections by looking to the diction ;
as, for instance, to foreign words :

On mules th' infection first began.

For perhaps he does not use οὐρῆας to signify *mules*,
but *guards*[8]. And in what he says of Dolon,

—— εἶδος μὲν ἔην κακός[9]——

—— of form unhappy

It may be said that εἶδος κακὸς does not signify a
body without symmetry, but a deformed face. For
the Cretans call a man with a good face εὐειδής.
And,

Ζωρότερον δὲ κέραιε ————[10]

For ζωρότερον may not mean *undiluted* wine, as for

[7] Il. X. 152. See Ritter.
[8] Il. A. 50. Zoilus thought the pestilence should have be-
gun with the men first.
[9] Il. K. 316. The objection of the critics is *supposed* to
have been, that an *ill-made* man could not be a good racer.
See Pope's note. Twining.
[10] Iliad ix. 267, 8.—Pope follows the common, and probably
the right, acceptation of the word. "Mix *purer* wine."—Aristotle's interpretation has not made its fortune with the critics.
He seems to have produced it rather as an exemplification of
the *sort* of answer which he is here considering, than as an
opinion in which he acquiesced himself. It was, probably, an
answer which *had* been given. The cavil, according to Plu-
tarch, came from *Zoilus*. [See the Symposiac Prob. of Plut.
v. 4, where this subject is discussed, and several other con-
jectural senses of the word Ζωρότερον are proposed.] Twining.

intemperate drinkers, but wine poured out rapidly.
But a thing is said metaphorically, as,   10 Metaphor.

> The other gods and men[11] ———
> Slept all the night.

And at the same time he says :

> Ἤτοι ὅτ' ἐς πέδιον τὸ Τρωικὸν ἀθρήσειεν
> Αὐλῶν συρίγγων θ' ὁμαδόν.———

For *all* is said metaphorically, instead of *many, all*[12]
being a *species* of *many*. And thus οἴη δ' ἄμμορος is
said of Orion metaphorically. For that which is
most known, is called *alone* or *sole*[13]. Objections also   11. Accent.
may be solved from accent, as Hippias the Thasian
solved the following passages :

> δίδομεν δέ οἱ [εὖχος ἀρέσθαι].

And,

> ——— τὸ μὲν οὐ καταπύθεται ὄμβρῳ[14].

Objections likewise may be solved by punctuation ;   12. Punctuation.
as in the following instance from Empedocles,

> Αἶψα δὲ θνήτ' ἐφύοντο, τὰ πρὶν μάθον ἀθάνατ' εἶναι,
> Ζωρά τε τὰ πρὶν κέκριτο.[15] ———

[11] Beginning of Il. ii.—*What* it was that wanted defence in
this passage, and that was to be taken metaphorically, we are
not told. That it was the representation of the *gods* as *sleeping*, is the most probable conjecture. This is somewhat soft-
ened by Mr. Pope's "*slumbered*." Homer says—" SLEPT *all
the night*,"—ευδον παννυχιοι. Twining.

[12] πάντες is a far-fetched notion from παννύχιοι. The author
has blundered between Il. B. 1., and Il. I. 1, and 11—13.
See Ritter.

[13] Il. xxi. 297, has δίδομεν δέ τοι εὖχος ἀρέσθαι, but the line,
as here quoted, is not found in Homer. See Ritter. Taylor observes: " It alludes to the order given by Jupiter to the dream in
Il. ii. to deceive Agamemnon. Here, if δίδομεν is read with
an accent in the antepenult, it will signify *damus*, and will imply that Jupiter promises Agamemnon glory from the battle ;
but if it is read with an accent in the penult, διδόμεν, so as to
be the infinitive Ionic, it will signify *dare*. It will therefore
imply that Jupiter orders the dream to *give the hope* of victory
to Agamemnon."

[14] If this is read with the circumflex on the οὖ, it will signify
that the oak became putrid by the rain, which is absurd; but
if it is read with an acute accent and spiritus lenis οὔ, it will
signify *not*, and will imply, that the oak was not rotted by the
rain. Taylor.

[15] The sense here depends on the punctuation. For if the

13. Ambiguity.

Or by ambiguous expressions, as [in Iliad, x.]

———— παρώχηκεν δὲ πλέων νυξ[16].

Night of two parts the greater share had waned,
But of her empire still a third remain'd.

14. Custom of diction.

For the word πλέων is ambiguous. Or objections may be answered from the custom of diction; as when wine is called κεκραμένον, mixed[17]; whence has been said,

———— Greaves of new-wrought tin.

And those that work on iron are called braziers[18]. Whence Ganymede is said

———— To pour out wine for Jove[19];   Il. 20.

15. Contraries.

though the gods do not drink wine. But this may also be metaphorically said. It is necessary, however, when a word appears to signify something of a contrary nature, to consider how many significations it may have in the passage before us; as,

———— τῇ ῥ᾽ ἔσχετο χάλκεον ἔγχος—

" There stuck the lance[20] :"————

For here the word stuck implies that the lance was impeded. Of how many different senses a word may admit, one may learn thus, by a contrary manner

comma is put after ζωρὰ in the second line, instead of πρὶν, the sense will be, " Immediately those things were made mortal which before had learnt to be immortal, and pure which before were mixed." But if the comma is put after πρὶν instead of ζωρὰ, the sense will be, " that those things which before were pure, were mixed." Taylor. But see Ritter's learned note.

[16] But the ambiguity is occasioned by the word πλέων, which may either signify more than, or the greater part of. Taylor. Il. Κ. 252.

Ἄστρα δὲ δὴ προβέβηκε, παρώχηκεν δὲ πλέων νύξ,
τῶν δύο μοιράων.

[17] " Ea potio quæ ex aqua et vino commixta est tamen vinum nominatur. Nove dictum φασιν εἶναι pro λέγουσιν." Ritter.

[18] " Schol. in Hom. Il. Τ. 283. παλαιὰ ἡ χρῆσις τοῦ χαλκὸν ὀνομάζειν τὸν σίδηρον. ἀμέλει καὶ χαλκέας τοὺς τὸν σίδηρον ἐργαζομένους. Ritter.

[19] Il. Υ. 234.

[20] Il. Υ. 272. This is consummate twaddle. See Twining and Ritter.

from what Glauco says[21], [when he asserts that]
" some men presuppose irrationally, and then reason
from their own decision: and, having once pronounced
their opinion, reprobate whatever is contrary to their
[preconceived] opinion." This was the case with respect to Icarius. For the multitude fancy that he was
a Laconian. On this supposition, therefore, it is absurd that Telemachus should not meet him, on his ar-
rival at Lacedæmon[22]. Perhaps, however, the truth
is as the Cephalenians say, viz. that Ulysses married
among them, and that Icadius, and not Icarius, [was
his father-in-law]. It is probable, therefore, that this 17.
objection is erroneous. In short, it is necessary to
refer the impossible either to the poetry, or to that
which is better, or to opinion. For, with respect to
poetry, probable impossibility is more eligible, than
the improbable and possible, and things should be
such as Zeuxis[23] painted. And also [we may refer
the impossible] to that which is better[24]: for it is necessary that the pattern should transcend those things
which are said to be irrational. The objection, also,
that something is irrational may be solved by saying,
that sometimes it is not irrational; for it is probable
that what is improbable may have happened. But 18.
with respect to the solution of apparent contraries,
these are to be considered in the same manner as

[21] This is most clumsily and indistinctly expressed.

[22] See Ritter.

[23] " In ancient days, while *Greece* was flourishing in liberty
and arts, a celebrated painter, [*Zeuxis*,] having drawn many
excellent pictures for a certain free state, and been generously
rewarded for his labours, at last made an offer to paint them a
Helen, as a *model* and *exemplar* of the most exquisite beauty.
The proposal was readily accepted, when the artist informed
them, that in order to draw *one* Fair, it was necessary he
should contemplate *many*. He demanded, therefore, a sight of
all their finest women. The state, to assist the work, assented
to his request. They were exhibited before him; he selected
the most beautiful; and from these formed his *Helen*, more
beautiful than them all."—Harris's Three Treatises, p. 216.
Twining.

[24] Improved nature, ideal beauty, etc., which, elsewhere, is
expressed by what *should be*. Twining. Ritter rightly supplies τὸ ἀδύνατον δεῖ ἀνάγειν.

elenchi[25] in arguments, if the same thing [is affirmed
or denied], and with respect to the same thing, and
after the same manner, and whether it is the same
person [who affirms and denies], and also with what
reference he speaks, and what a wise man would un-

19.   derstand from his words[26]. The reprehension [of
When   poets] on the score of improbability[27] and vicious
reprehen-
sion is   manners will be right, through which it is shown,
correct. that they have without any necessity devised something irrational. Thus irrationality is used [with-
out any necessity] by Euripides in his Ægeus, and
viciousness, in the character of Menelaus, in his
20. Sum- Orestes. The reprehensions, therefore, may be de-
mary.   rived from five species. For they are either made
because impossibilities are introduced, or absurdities,
or things of evil tendency, or contraries, or as errors
committed against the rectitude of art. But the solutions may be surveyed from the above-mentioned
number; for they are twelve.[28]]

CHAP. XXVI.

1. Re-   ONE may, however, question whether epic or tragic
spective
merits of   imitation is the more excellent. For if that imita-
tragic and tion is the better which is less troublesome to the
epic imi-
tation.   spectator, and such an imitation pertains to better
spectators, that which imitates every thing is evidently attended with molestation. For, as if the
spectators will not perceive what is acted without
the addition of much movement[1], they make great

[25] i. e. confutations.

[26] I have followed Ritter, who has done much for this awkward heap of tautologies.

[27] Surely the words καὶ ἀλογία καὶ μοχθηρία are corrupt or
interpolated.

[28] The reader who regards his own ease, will, I believe, do
well to take this for granted. If, however, he has any desire
to try the experiment, he may read my NOTE on this passage;
and I wish it may answer to him. Twining.

[1] Though Aristotle instances in *gesture* only, the objection,

gesticulations; just as bad players on the flute turn
themselves round, when it is requisite to imitate the
action of the discus; or when they sing of Scylla, draw
to themselves[2] the coryphæus, or leader of the band.
Such, then, is tragedy, as the modern actors are in
the estimation of their predecessors[3]. Hence, Mynis-
cus called Callipides an ape, in consequence of carrying his imitation to a great excess. And there was
also a similar opinion respecting Pindar [the player].
But as these latter actors are to the former, so is the
whole art of tragedy to the epopee. They say, therefore, that the epopee is calculated for hearers of the
better sort, on which account it does not require
scenery; but that tragedy is calculated for the vulgar. Hence, tragic imitation, which is troublesome
to the spectator, will evidently be inferior to epic
imitation.

2. Complaints respecting actors.

In the first place, however, this accusation does
not pertain to the poet, but the actor; since it is
possible in reciting epic poetry to overdo action, as
Sosistratus did, and singing likewise, as Mnastheus
of Opus did. In the next place, neither is all motion
to be despised, since neither is every kind of dancing,

3. But the whole question rather pertains to the actor than the poet.

no doubt, extended to the *whole* imitative representation of the
theatre, including the *stage* and *scenery*, by which *place* is
imitated, and the *dresses*, which are necessary to complete the
imitation of the *persons*.   Twining.
   [2] "Ελκοντες τὸν Κορυφαῖον—To imitate *Scylla*,—" naves in
saxa *trahentem*," as Virgil has expressed it. But it is not easy
to see how the performer, at least while he was playing, could
well spare a hand for this operation.—This was even worse
than what we call *humouring* a catch; when, for instance, a
singer who is performing Purcell's " *Fie, nay prithee, John*,"
—thinks it necessary to collar his neighbour.   Twining.
   Sheridan has burlesqued this habit of "suiting the action"
with admirable humour in " the Critic." Sir Christopher Hat-
ton turning out his toes, Lord Burleigh shaking his head, and
Tilburnia going mad in white satin, are among the best of his
innumerable *facetiæ* on the subject.   Compare also " the Re-
hearsal," Act 1, where Bayes instructs the Thunder and Light-
ning how to express their noisy and rapid powers by suitable
action.
   [3] The " decline of the drama," then, was a subject of complaint at Athens, as well as in London.

but only that which is bad; and hence Callipedes was blamed, as others now are for imitating light women [4]. Further still, tragedy, in the same manner as the epopee, may fulfil its purpose without gesture; for by reading, it is manifest what kind of thing it is. If, therefore, it is in other respects better, it is not necessary that it should be accompanied [by motion and gesture]. In the next place, tragedy has every thing which the epopee possesses. For it may use metre, and it has also music and scenery, as no small parts, through which the pleasure it produces is most apparent. To which may be added, that it possesses perspicuity, both when it is read, and when it is acted. The end, too, of its imitation is confined in less extended limits. For being crowded into a narrower compass, it becomes more pleasing than if it were diffused through a long period of time. Thus, for instance, if one were to put the Œdipus of Sophocles into as many verses as the Iliad, [it would be less pleasing]. Again, the imitation of the epopee has less unity [than tragic imitation]; of which this is an indication, that from any kind of [epic] imitation many tragedies may be produced. Hence, if he who writes an epic poem should choose a fable perfectly one, the poem would necessarily either appear short, as if curtailed, or if it should be accompanied with length of metre, it would seem to be languid [5]. But if he should compose one fable from many fables, I mean, if the poem should consist of many actions, it would not possess unity. Thus, the Iliad and Odyssey contain many such parts, which of themselves possess magnitude, though these poems are composed, as much as possible, in the most excellent

4. Reasons for the superiority of tragedy.

5.

6.

---

[4] Taylor has gone fearfully astray in his version, "for not imitating free women"! The negative particle belongs to the adjective. Twining observes: "as no *actresses* were admitted on the Greek stage, their capital *actors* must frequently have appeared in female parts, such as *Electra, Iphigenia, Medea,* etc. This is sufficiently proved by many passages of ancient authors; and among others, by a remarkable story of Polus, an eminent Greek Tragic actor, told by *Aulus Gellius.*"

[5] ὑδαρῆ, *milk-and-waterish.*

manner, and are most eminently the imitation of one
action.   If, therefore, tragedy excels in all these 7.
particulars, and besides this, in the work of art, (for
neither tragic nor epic imitation ought to produce a
casual pleasure, but that which has been stated,) it
is evident that it will be more excellent than the
epopee, in consequence of attaining its end in a
greater degree.   And thus much concerning tragedy, 8.
and the epopee, as to themselves, their species, and
their parts, their number, and their difference, what
the causes are of their being good or bad, and also
concerning the objections which may be made to
them, and the solutions of the objections.

GREAT BOOKS IN PHILOSOPHY PAPERBACK SERIES

ETHICS

Aristotle—*The Nicomachean Ethics*	$8.95
Marcus Aurelius—*Meditations*	5.95
Jeremy Bentham—*The Principles of Morals and Legislation*	8.95
John Dewey—*The Moral Writings of John Dewey, Revised Edition*	
(edited by James Gouinlock)	10.95
Epictetus—*Enchiridion*	4.95
Immanuel Kant—*Fundamental Principles of the Metaphysic of Morals*	5.95
John Stuart Mill—*Utilitarianism*	5.95
George Edward Moore—*Principia Ethica*	8.95
Friedrich Nietzsche—*Beyond Good and Evil*	8.95
Plato—*Protagoras, Philebus*, and *Gorgias*	7.95
Bertrand Russell—*Bertrand Russell On Ethics, Sex, and Marriage*	
(edited by Al Seckel)	19.95
Arthur Schopenhauer—*The Wisdom of Life* and *Counsels and Maxims*	6.95
Benedict de Spinoza—*Ethics* and *The Improvement of the Understanding*	9.95

SOCIAL AND POLITICAL PHILOSOPHY

Aristotle—*The Politics*	7.95
Francis Bacon—*Essays*	6.95
Mikhail Bakunin—*The Basic Bakunin: Writings, 1869–1871*	
(translated and edited by Robert M. Cutler)	11.95
Edmund Burke—*Reflections on the Revolution in France*	7.95
John Dewey—*Freedom and Culture*	10.95
G. W. F. Hegel—*The Philosophy of History*	9.95
G. W. F. Hegel—*Philosophy of Right*	9.95
Thomas Hobbes—*The Leviathan*	7.95
Sidney Hook—*Paradoxes of Freedom*	9.95
Sidney Hook—*Reason, Social Myths, and Democracy*	11.95
John Locke—*Second Treatise on Civil Government*	5.95
Niccolo Machiavelli—*The Prince*	5.95
Karl Marx (with Friedrich Engels)—*The German Ideology,*	
including *Theses on Feuerbach and Introduction to the*	
Critique of Political Economy	10.95
Karl Marx—*The Poverty of Philosophy*	7.95
Karl Marx/Friedrich Engels—*The Economic and Philosophic Manuscripts of 1844*	
and *The Communist Manifesto*	6.95
John Stuart Mill—*Considerations on Representative Government*	6.95
John Stuart Mill—*On Liberty*	5.95
John Stuart Mill—*On Socialism*	7.95
John Stuart Mill—*The Subjection of Women*	5.95
Friedrich Nietzsche—*Thus Spake Zarathustra*	9.95
Thomas Paine—*Common Sense*	5.95
Thomas Paine—*Rights of Man*	7.95
Plato—*Lysis, Phaedrus*, and *Symposium*	6.95
Plato—*The Republic*	9.95
Jean-Jacques Rousseau—*The Social Contract*	5.95
Mary Wollstonecraft—*A Vindication of the Rights of Men*	5.95
Mary Wollstonecraft—*A Vindication of the Rights of Women*	6.95

METAPHYSICS/EPISTEMOLOGY

Aristotle—*De Anima*	6.95
Aristotle—*The Metaphysics*	9.95
George Berkeley—*Three Dialogues Between Hylas and Philonous*	5.95
René Descartes—*Discourse on Method* and *The Meditations*	6.95
John Dewey—*How We Think*	10.95
John Dewey—*The Influence of Darwin on Philosophy and Other Essays*	11.95
Epicurus—*The Essential Epicurus: Letters, Principal Doctrines,*	
Vatican Sayings, and Fragments	
(translated, and with an introduction, by Eugene O'Connor)	5.95
Sidney Hook—*The Quest for Being*	11.95
David Hume—*An Enquiry Concerning Human Understanding*	6.95
David Hume—*Treatise of Human Nature*	9.95
William James—*The Meaning of Truth*	11.95
William James—*Pragmatism*	7.95
Immanuel Kant—*Critique of Practical Reason*	7.95
Immanuel Kant—*Critique of Pure Reason*	9.95
Gottfried Wilhelm Leibniz—*Discourse on Method* and the *Monadology*	6.95
John Locke—*An Essay Concerning Human Understanding*	9.95
Charles S. Peirce—*The Essential Writings*	
(edited by Edward C. Moore, preface by Richard Robin)	10.95
Plato—*The Euthyphro, Apology, Crito, and Phaedo*	5.95
Bertrand Russell—*The Problems of Philosophy*	8.95
George Santayana—*The Life of Reason*	9.95
Sextus Empiricus—*Outlines of Pyrrhonism*	8.95

PHILOSOPHY OF RELIGION

Marcus Tullius Cicero—*The Nature of the Gods* and *On Divination*	6.95
Ludwig Feuerbach—*The Essence of Christianity*	8.95
David Hume—*Dialogues Concerning Natural Religion*	5.95
John Locke—*A Letter Concerning Toleration*	5.95
Lucretius—*On the Nature of Things*	7.95
John Stuart Mill—*Three Essays on Religion*	7.95
Thomas Paine—*The Age of Reason*	13.95
Bertrand Russell—*Bertrand Russell On God and Religion* (edited by Al Seckel)	19.95

ESTHETICS

Aristotle—*The Poetics*	5.95
Aristotle—*Treatise on Rhetoric*	7.95

GREAT MINDS PAPERBACK SERIES

ECONOMICS

Charlotte Perkins Gilman—*Women and Economics: A Study of the*	
Economic Relation between Women and Men	11.95
John Maynard Keynes—*The General Theory of Employment, Interest, and Money*	11.95
Thomas R. Malthus—*An Essay on the Principle of Population*	14.95
Alfred Marshall—*Principles of Economics*	11.95
David Ricardo—*Principles of Political Economy and Taxation*	10.95
Adam Smith—*Wealth of Nations*	9.95
Thorstein Veblen—*Theory of the Leisure Class*	11.95

RELIGION

Thomas Henry Huxley—*Agnosticism and Christianity and Other Essays*	10.95
Ernest Renan—*The Life of Jesus*	11.95
Voltaire—*A Treatise on Toleration and Other Essays*	8.95

SCIENCE

Nicolaus Copernicus—*On the Revolutions of Heavenly Spheres*	8.95
Charles Darwin—*The Descent of Man*	18.95
Charles Darwin—*The Origin of Species*	10.95
Albert Einstein—*Relativity*	8.95
Michael Faraday—*The Forces of Matter*	8.95
Galileo Galilei—*Dialogues Concerning Two New Sciences*	9.95
Ernst Haeckel—*The Riddle of the Universe*	11.95
William Harvey—*On the Motion of the Heart and Blood in Animals*	9.95
Julian Huxley—*Evolutionary Humanism*	10.95
Edward Jenner—*Vaccination against Smallpox*	5.95
Johannes Kepler—*Epitome of Copernican Astronomy* and *Harmonies of the World*	8.95
Isaac Newton—*The Principia*	14.95
Louis Pasteur and Joseph Lister—*Germ Theory and Its Application to Medicine and On the Antiseptic Principle of the Practice of Surgery*	7.95
Alfred Russel Wallace—*Island Life*	16.95

HISTORY

Edward Gibbon—*On Christianity*	9.95
Herodotus—*The History*	13.95
Thucydides—*History of the Peloponnesian War*	15.95
Andrew D. White—*A History of the Warfare of Science with Theology in Christendom*	19.95

SOCIOLOGY

Emile Durkheim—*Ethics and the Sociology of Morals* (translated with an introduction by Robert T. Hall)	8.95

CRITICAL ESSAYS

Desiderius Erasmus—*The Praise of Folly*	9.95
Jonathan Swift—*A Modest Proposal and Other Satires* (with an introduction by George R. Levine)	8.95
H. G. Wells—*The Conquest of Tme* (with an introduction by Martin Gardner)	8.95

(Prices subject to change without notice.)

ORDER FORM

Prometheus Books
59 John Glenn Drive • Amherst, New York 14228–2197
Telephone: (716) 691–0133

Phone Orders (24 hours):
Toll free (800) 421–0351 • FAX (716) 691–0137
Email: PBooks6205@aol.com

Ship to: _____

Address _____

_____

City _____

County (*N.Y. State Only*) _____

Telephone _____

Prometheus Acct. # _____

❑ Payment enclosed (or)

Charge to ❑ VISA ❑ MasterCard

A/C: ❑❑❑❑❑❑❑❑❑❑❑❑❑❑❑❑❑❑❑❑

Exp. Date _____ / _____

Signature _____